The Practical Guide to Japanese Signs [1st part]

The Practical Guide to
Japanese Signs

1st part

Especially for Newcomers

Tae Moriyama

trans. by Jeffrey Cohen

KODANSHA INTERNATIONAL
Tokyo, New York & San Francisco

Distributed in the United States by Kodansha International/USA Ltd. through Harper & Row, Publishers, Inc., 10 East 53rd Street, New York, New York 10022.

Published by Kodansha International Ltd., 2–2 Otowa 1-chome, Bunkyo-ku, Tokyo 112 and Kodansha International/USA Ltd., 10 East 53rd Street, New York, New York 10022 and the Hearst Bldg., 5 Third Street, San Francisco, California 94103.
Printed in Japan.
First edition, 1987   ISBN4–7700–1290–X in Japan

Library of Congress Cataloging-in-Publication Data
Moriyama, Tae, 1927–
    The practical guide to Japanese signs.
    Includes indexes.
    Contents: 1st pt. Especially for Newcomers. 2nd pt. Making Life Easier
    1. Japanese language–glossaries, vocabularies, etc. 2. Signs and signboards–Japan. I. Title.
PL685.M65 1986   895.6'81   86–45788
ISBN 0–87011–790–4

Contents

	Preface	7
	Introduction	9
1.	Stations and Trains	19
2.	Ticket Machines, Trains	37
3.	Ticket Machines, Subways	42
4.	Station Windows	48
5.	Taxis	52
6.	Buses	55
7.	Airports	57
8.	Inns	60
9.	One Night, Two Meals	64
10.	Baths	66
11.	Natural Features	71
12.	Shintō and Buddhism	75
13.	Statue and Garden	79
14.	Castles and Museums	82
15.	Geography	86
16.	Numbers	90
17.	Noodles	93
18.	Restaurant and *Shokudō*	99

19.	Grilled Chicken and Raw Fish	104
20.	A Glassful, a Bottle	107
21.	Open for Business	110
22.	Post Office	115
23.	Basics of Banking	120
24.	Bank Machines	125
25.	Utilities and Taxes	132
26.	Body Shops	136
27.	Clothes	139
28.	Some Luxuries	141
29.	Some Hobbies	145
30.	Food for Your Table	149
	Appendix: Vocabulary Building	154
	Bibliography	169
	Pronunciation Index	170
	Index	177

Preface

My purpose in writing this book is to familiarize the reader with the Chinese characters that are of most immediate importance for anyone living in Japan. Like so many of my students, you must have been awed by written Japanese when you first arrived in this country. There are ways to survive this particular cultural shock and I hope this book and its companion volume will help you to do so.

It all began early in 1978 when Ann Nakano, a *Mainichi Daily News* reporter and a student of mine, suggested a series of articles about Chinese characters commonly seen in signs. The idea interested me, and in April of that year I started a weekly column in the *Mainichi Daily News*. It was called "Signs Will Tell You" and I expected that it would take no more than half a year for the subject to be exhausted. However, once I started writing about signs I realized there were lots of words and situations to be explained. It wasn't long, either, before letters and telephone calls began to come in from readers urging me to continue. There was a short break at one point, but by the time it was all over I had written 203 "Signs Will Tell You" columns, published over a period of more than five years.

Later came requests to have the columns brought together in book form, which presented a number of options. Some were easy to deal with. For example, since I had been writing for a newspaper, the style had had to be one readily accessible to the general reader. It was not difficult to decide that the book, too, should retain this quality. Anyone, even people who have no knowledge of Japanese, should be able to dip into it more or less at random and come up with an item or two of useful or interesting information. Students of Japanese, on the other hand, will find that because of its practical orientation, it adds a dimension to the study of Chinese characters that is sometimes lacking in classroom instruction.

Between 1978 and the present many things, including train fares and postal rates and the design of ticket vending machines and automatic teller machines and so on, have changed, some more than others. Naturally, this required revision and updating, in addition to which I decided to add some signs not covered in the columns and make other changes, necessitating an overall reorganization and rewriting of the material. One result was that we ended up with an estimate that it would take around four hundred pages to get everything into one book. This lead us to decide that two volumes would better serve the purpose. Done this way, the books could be kept small enough to slip into pocket or purse for handy reference and, hopefully, the price could be kept more affordable.

The Introduction that follows gives more particulars about Chinese characters and the book itself, so I would like to close this preface by expressing my deepest appreciation to the people whose invaluable cooperation has done so much to make the original columns and this book possible: Akiyuki Konishi, Editorial Director, *Mainichi Daily News*; Ann Nakano, who is now a free lance journalist; the translator; and my editor and the executives of Kodansha International.

Introduction

At the very beginning it should be made clear what this book is and what it is not. It has been written to make life easier for people with little or no understanding of Japanese by offering them a way of deciphering the myriad signs, directions, instructions, labels and so on that are constantly encountered in daily life. Although I have included a lot of information about Chinese characters, this book by itself will not make the reader a scholar of written Japanese. In fact, the would-be scholar of *kanji*, the building blocks of Japanese words, will face the same problems I have had to deal with, a brief discussion of which follows.

Based on archaeological findings, it is believed that this type of writing first appeared in China between the fourteenth and eleventh centuries B.C. In Japanese we call the characters *kanji*, *kan* being an old name for "China" and *ji* meaning "character." A modern and more precise way to refer to them is as Sino-Japanese characters, since they have been used in Japan for centuries and many have undergone modification in one way or another.

At one time there was an astronomical number of characters available for use in China. In 1716 during the Ch'ing dynasty, a forty-two-volume character dictionary, the *K'ang-hsi tzu-tien*, was completed, based on dictionaries compiled through the ages and containing over forty-two thousand characters, although it is estimated that not more than one quarter of the total number was in actual use at that particular time. This tremendous compendium is still considered to be THE character dictionary, even today.

In 1922, to facilitate public education, Chinese authorities not only reduced the number of kanji to be used (to twenty-two thousand) but simplified the forms of characters to a great extent.

It is believed that kanji were systematically introduced into

Japan around the fifth or sixth century A.D. Subsequently, the number of imported Chinese characters continued to increase, for Chinese literature and other disciplines have been a notable influence on Japanese culture.

In modern times, from the beginning of the Meiji period (1868) until the end of World War II, the number of kanji in general use in Japanese totaled around thirty-six hundred, the most frequently used two thousand having both Chinese and Japanese readings. Presently, the number of kanji selected for the basic educational curriculum and use in publications for the general public is limited to the 1945 Jōyō ("common use") Kanji. This guideline was established by the Ministry of Education in March, 1981, and shows rather few changes from the previous list of 1850 characters that was adopted in 1946.

So there are reasons for the difficulty of studying about kanji—their long history and great number, both of which imply changes and revisions as time passes, and the fact that they originated in one country and are used in another country. (There are kanji of Japanese origin, but the total number is not very great.) Here, I would like to mention two other factors, the readings and the origins of individual characters.

A reading of a character similar to the Chinese pronunciation at the time it was introduced into Japan is called an *on* reading. An indigenous Japanese reading assigned to a kanji to accord with a particular meaning is called a *kun* reading. There are some kanji with only one reading, either *on* or *kun*, but most have acquired both kinds of pronunciation.

To complicate matters a bit more, linguistic changes in Chinese, as well as regional differences, have led to there being two or more *on* readings for many kanji. Similarly, a single kanji may have two or more kun readings, with the same, related or dissimilar meanings. There is one very commonly used character—*sei*, one of the basic meanings of which is "life"—with altogether sixteen different readings, more than any other Sino-Japanese character.

As can be seen by leafing through any kanji dictionary, multiple theories of origin are offered for many characters. In some cases, original meanings have been lost, and it is impossible to be absolutely certain of the original meaning. In other cases, pronunciations have been grafted onto characters, sometimes by borrowing from another character. In still other cases, a character has taken on new meanings, possibly using old pronunciations. For this and similar reasons, to flatly state that one theory of origin is correct and another is not is, in many instances, simply not possible. As may be imagined, in writing this book I had quite a time choosing between conflicting theories. Needless to say, introducing all the theories for all the characters covered here would only overwhelm the reader. What gave me the greatest trouble was trying to imagine the original shapes of certain simplified characters. In the end I opted for the explanation I felt would be most helpful to the reader in remembering the kanji in its present form.

Given the complexity of discussing Sino-Japanese characters (there are more factors than those already mentioned), one may well ask, is it possible to learn to recognize them? The answer is, of course, yes. But if the answer is yes, the next legitimate question is how.

Japanese children are expected to learn all the Jōyō Kanji by the time they graduate from junior high school. This turns out to be quite a demanding task. Even I have unpleasant memories of being forced to memorize kanji when I was young. To tell the truth, it was not until I was an adult that I rediscovered kanji by looking at them from a fresh viewpoint.

Take, for example, the two kanji *wasu(reru)*, "to forget," and *isoga(shii)*, "busy." Both are combinations of the same two elements, which mean *shin*, "heart," and *na(kunaru)*, "to lose." In *wasu(reru)* these are written one above the other, in *na(kunaru)* side by side. For some reason, perhaps because I thought of myself as a person who easily loses heart, this came like a revelation to me, and I felt I could understand the people of a thousand years B.C., who must have had a similar feeling when they invented this type of writing and saw that it actually worked.

As you will see little by little, we can find lots of examples of interesting word formation: "woman" and "house" combined to mean "bride"; "woman" and "good" to mean "daughter"; "rice field" and "strength" to mean "man"; the radicals "to say" and "tongue" to mean "to talk"; the "water" radical and the "tongue" radical to mean "to live."

In short, once one realizes there is a logic behind a great number of kanji, learning them becomes a mere challenge, not just a painful exercise in rote learning. I say this with confidence, as it was definitely true in my own case. I have wished many times that I had made this discovery sooner. Fortunately, it is not too late to hope that this book will help you to find a shortcut to learning the basic meanings of kanji while enjoying yourself in the process.

One thing to keep in mind is that Chinese characters originated as pictures. Looking at the first kanji in the book, which is pronounced *eki* and means "station," we find that it consists of a character meaning "horse" on the left side and one meaning "measuring stick" on the right. If this makes you wonder what these two characters have in common with a train station, think of it like this. Before modern transportation the horse was one basic means of traveling along the highways from one inn town to another. Seen this way, the character for station now consists of two basic concepts: a device used to measure distance and the means for covering that distance.

The word *ginkō*, "bank," is made up of two kanji, one meaning silver and the other "to go." A bank is a place where money goes, surely, but wouldn't the kanji meaning "gold" be even more appropriate than the one for silver? Perhaps, but in Japan during the Edo period (1603–1867), silver, rather than gold, was the more common medium of exchange. As you can see in this example, many kanji are miniature mirrors of history and culture.

Looking at it another way, while the factors mentioned so far provide background information, they need not automatically become memory loads at the first stage of learning kanji. For example, this book naturally includes both on and kun readings, but they are not labeled as such, because it is not a matter of practical importance at this stage. You can easily learn how to recognize which is which later on, if the necessity arises. Also, I have not given all the readings for each character discussed in this book; I have generally included the most common readings, along with a few others for illustrative purposes.

The first use this book will be put to is the deciphering of signs. Beyond that, I do recommend that you familiarize yourself with kanji. The more you make a habit of this, the more interesting it becomes. Noticing shop signs as you walk down the street, searching for kanji you already know in the ads on trains and buses, and simply picking out familiar kanji on product labels while shopping should help to close the gap between you and this whole new way of writing. Learning even a few kanji will help you to enjoy life in Japan a little bit more.

Except for the very simplest, kanji are generally a combination of various elements. One way to give a boost to the learning process is to be able to recognize elements.

To look up a kanji in a dictionary, first you must find the radical included in the particular character. (Some kanji are both radicals and independent characters.) There is always a list of radicals at the beginning of any kanji dictionary. The dictionary I always refer to lists 250 radicals. Not all of these appear in Jōyō Kanji, and the number of radicals actually in use today totals around 240.

It is not necessary to learn the names of all the radicals, but as a minimum, it would be a good idea to learn the eight different types given below, with some examples of each, since they are extremely common. It is best to learn and use the Japanese terms by which they are identified, the English translations being very rarely of any practical use whatsoever.

1. 木	*kihen*	2. 女	*onnahen*	3. 言	*gonben*
4. 氵	*mizuhen/sanzui*	5. 亻	*ninben*	6. 口	*kuchihen*
7. 梅	*ume*	8. 嫁	*yome*	9. 話	*hana(su)*
10. 海	*umi*	11. 休	*yasu(mu)*	12. 呼	*yo(bu)*

1. *Hen*: These radicals make up the left side of certain kanji

which consist of a right and a left side but have neither a top nor a bottom part. Commonly seen *hen* include *kihen*, *onnahen*, *gonben*, *mizuhen/sanzui*, *ninben* and *kuchihen* (Figs. 1–6). These are seen, respectively, in the characters: *ume*, "plum"; *yome*, "bride"; *hana(su)*, "to speak"; *umi*, "ocean"; *yasu(mu)*, "to rest"; and *yo-(bu)*, "to call" (Figs. 7–12).

13. 青 ao-zukuri   14. 力 *chikara-zukuri*   15. 斤 ono-zukuri

16. 寺 tera-zukuri   17. 晴 ha(reru)   18. 助 tasu(keru)

19. 新 atara(shii)   20. 時 toki

2. *Tsukuri(-zukuri)*: These radicals make up the right side of certain kanji which consist of a right side and a left side but have neither a top nor a bottom part. Examples of common *tsukuri* include *ao-zukuri*, *chikara-zukuri*, *ono-zukuri* and *tera-zukuri* (Figs. 13–16). These are employed in the characters for *ha(reru)*, "to clear up"; *tasu(keru)*, "to help"; *atara(shii)*, "new"; and *toki*, "time," respectively (Figs. 17–20).

21. ⺾ kusakanmuri   22. 雨 amekanmuri   23. 宀 ukanmuri

24. ⺮ takekanmuri   25. 花 hana   26. 電 den

27. 家 ie   28. 節 setsu

3. *Kanmuri*: These radicals make up the top part of certain kanji. Common *kanmuri* are called *kusakanmuri*, *amekanmuri*, *ukanmuri* and *takekanmuri* (Figs. 21–24) and are found respectively in the kanji for *hana*, "flower"; *den*, "electricity"; *ie*, "house"; and *setsu*, "season" (Figs. 25–28).

29. 灬 renga   30. 貝 kai   31. 心 *shita-gokoro*

32. 熱 netsu   33. 買 ka(u)   34. 忘 wasu(reru)

4. *Ashi*: These radicals make up the bottom part of certain kanji. Three common *ashi* are called *renga*, *kai* and *shita-gokoro* (Figs. 29–31). One of these is used in writing the kanji *netsu*, "heat"; *ka(u)*, "to buy"; and *wasu(reru)*, "to forget" (Figs. 32–34).

35. 厂 *gan-dare*   36. 广 *ma-dare*   37. 疒 *yamai-dare*

38. 原 *hara*   39. 広 *hiro(i)*   40. 病 *yamai*

5. *Tare(-dare)*: These cliff shaped radicals run along the top and down the left side of the kanji in which they appear. Three of the common *tare* radicals are *gan-dare*, *ma-dare*, and *yamai-dare* (Figs. 35–37), seen respectively in the characters *hara*, "field"; *hiro(i)*, "wide"; and *yamai*, "sickness" (Figs. 38–40).

41. 辶 *shinnyō*   42. 廴 *ennyō*   43. 走 *sōnyō*

44. 道 *michi*   45. 建 *ta(teru)*   46. 越 *ko(eru)*

6. *Nyō*: There are only three of these radicals and they are located on the left side of the kanji, where they form partial enclosures. They are known as *shinnyō*, *ennyō* and *sōnyō* (Figs. 41–43). Kanji in which they are found are *michi*, "road"; *ta(teru)*, "to build"; and *ko(eru)*, "to go across" (Figs. 44–46).

47. 囗 *kuni-gamae*   48. 門 *mon-gamae*   49. 冂 *dō-gamae*

50. 国 *kuni*   51. 間 *ma*   52. 円 *en*

7. *Kamae(-gamae)*: These radicals surround one or more other elements to form a character. Three commonly seen *kamae* are *kuni-gamae*, *mon-gamae* and *dō-gamae* (Figs. 47–49). These radicals appear in the kanji *kuni*, "country"; *ma*, "space"; and *en*, "yen," respectively (Figs 50–52).

53. ⺍ *hachi-gashira*   54. 癶 *hatsu-gashira*

55. 公 *ōyake*   56. 発 *ha(tsu)*

8. *Kashira(-gashira)*: Similar to the *kanmuri* radicals, *kashira* make up the top part of kanji. Two common *kashira* are *hachi-gashira* and *hatsu-gashira* (Figs. 53–54). They are seen respectively in the kanji *ōyake*, "public," and *ha(tsu)*, "to depart" (Figs. 55–56).

All the radicals mentioned above, with the exception of *tsukuri*, suggest the meaning of the kanji given as examples to a certain extent. Seeing such relationships and familiarizing yourself with them should turn out to be quite beneficial. Once you know that characters incorporating *kihen* include the names of trees and various things made of or related to wood, and that those with the *kusakanmuri* radical include characters which have to do with grass, plants and flowers, the logic of the writing system becomes a little more apparent.

Anyone compiling a book of this sort faces a dilemma. Ideally, there should be a way of locating a character in the book when nothing is known about it except its appearance. The two usual ways of doing this are by using the radical system or by stroke count, that is, counting the number of strokes needed to write the character. As we have seen, the former involves well over two hundred radicals, so it is hardly a shortcut for beginners. Similarly, learning to count strokes quickly and accurately requires understanding how kanji are written and takes a certain amount of time and practice before one becomes proficient. It also has the drawback that one might have to look through dozens of characters all having, say, nine strokes before finding the one desired.

What I have done is link my discussions to fairly narrow and easily identifiable situations and their signs, starting in the *lst Part* with public transportation and going on through sightseeing to restaurants, numbers, the post office and banks to a few types of well frequented shops. In the *2nd Part*, where I have had the longer term resident rather than the newcomer in mind, I have gone into things like emergencies, house hunting, medical services, certain traditional Japanese food and drink, driving and so on—situations less often encountered, but still in the realm of the everyday. The reader can easily find the situation he or she is interested in by scanning the book or by referring to the table of contents or the indices. For those times when the pronunciation of a word is known, there is a separate index of Japanese words and, if important for some reason, individual syllables.

In describing signs and other information seen in a certain place, it has not been possible to record each and every minute detail. Were one to go to the extreme of trying to cover all the station and train signs throughout the country, or every variation in automatic teller machines, etc., a book of a thousand pages would not be long enough. Therefore, I have concentrated on basic information and key words, which are often found in more than one situation. An obvious example is *otona*, "adult," a word to know when buying train tickets, but also when buying other tickets and in other situations. Again, having learned the kanji for *kaisō*, "out of service," as applied to taxis, you will recognize this sign, meaning the same thing, on trains and buses. Or by knowing that *futsū* identifies a local train, you will be familiar with its basic meaning of "ordinary" and be prepared for "ordinary" savings accounts and even certain "ordinary" offerings on a menu. You will find many opportunities for this type of transference from situation to situation.

It will soon become apparent that characters are building blocks. Just as a radical may appear in only a few or a great number of kanji, the kanji in turn may combine with a few or a great number of other kanji to form new words. It is for this reason that I have included the vocabulary-building appendix, choosing to the extent possible words that are made up entirely of kanji in this book (if such a word is also common and useful), terms that are representative of a character's meaning, or items that will, sooner or later, prove useful in daily life. There is no need to rush to make use of the appendix, but once you begin to get accustomed to this way of writing, you may find it an interesting, even enjoyable, place to browse for new information or confirmation of hunches you may have.

Finally, I would like to mention the *hiragana* and *katakana* syllabaries. In these phonemic systems of writing, basically one symbol (or one regular size plus one half size symbol) represents one syllable. *Hiragana* is used to write certain words and as a sort of mortar to cement the kanji building blocks into grammatical structures. *Katakana*'s principal use is in writing the thousands of loanwords in Japanese which come from languages other than Chinese, but Japanese words are to a limited extent written in *katakana* for a few specific purposes (domestic telegrams, for instance). These syllabaries are beyond the scope of this book (there are several good manuals for learning them), but since *kana* appear in signs and, especially, advertisements, the symbols and their pronunciations are given on the inside covers of this book for ready reference.

1

Stations and Trains

One of the most important aspects of everyday life in Japan is transportation. To make it as easy as possible for the newcomer to get around in this country, I have decided to give the basic orientation on this subject in the very first chapters of this book.

Although you will be able to find some place names and the like written in the English alphabet in large cities, once you are out in the country this will seldom be the case. So it is advisable for you to have the key words and phrases down pat before traveling around Japan on your own.

If you use the trains, as most of us do, you have probably come across many of the more common signs already and, perhaps, had trouble with them. Included among the signs to be recognized first are signs pointing out the four directions, signs meaning entrance and exit, those identifying train lines, those that tell you how to use the ticket vending machines and so on.

Fortunately, most signs you will see at train stations, bus stops and airports consist of common characters. Once you can understand these signs your life in Japan will be that much easier.

1. 駅 *eki*

This is the character for *eki*, "station" (Fig. 1). Since there are very few bus stations in Japan, it is all but synonymous with train station, but the same character with the same meaning will be met with at subway and ropeway and cable railway stations, too.

The radical on the left is the character *uma*, "horse," while the part on the right has been interpreted in many ways. It has imaginatively been described as a man leaning on a shovel. What's certain is that it is the character for *shaku*, an old unit of length. This and another meaning of this kanji, "measuring stick," suggest distance. In the old days, the distance between *shukuba* (villages which consisted almost entirely of hostelries) was covered on horseback as one alternative to walking. Shizuoka and Odawara, two stations on the Tokaido Line southwest of Tokyo, are good examples of former *shukuba* where travelers stopped to rest and horses were rented. (It should be noted that the right part of this character was formerly written with a more complicated element meaning "succession" or "change.")

2. ⌣ → ⊔ → 口 *kuchi*

Perhaps the one kanji most frequently seen at stations is *kuchi* (*-guchi*), meaning "mouth." This character originated from the crude drawing of a mouth (Fig. 2). It was simplified over the years to the shape shown in the middle picture and was then squared off to its final form.

3. 人 → 人 → 入   入口   *iri-guchi*

4. ⇞ → ⇞ → 出   出口   *de-guchi*

5. 改札口   *kaisatsu-guchi*

There are lots of words in which it is combined with other characters. For example, the words for "exit" and "entrance" are formed by combining the characters meaning "to go in" or "to go out," respectively, with the character for "mouth." The character for "to go in" was derived from the shape of the entrance of a house (Fig. 3), while the one for "to go out" depicts growing or "coming out." In figure 4 you can see the grass coming out of the ground.

"Exit" is read *de-guchi*, and "entrance" as *iri-guchi*. The final combination of characters shown here indicates the ticket gate at any station. It is read *kaisatsu-guchi* (Fig. 5).

6. *higashi* 東口 *higashi-guchi*

7. *minami* 南口 *minami-guchi*

At larger stations there are many exits and entrances, and, not surprisingly, at one station after another you will meet with north, south, east, west or central entrances and exits. Of course, local place names are much in evidence too.

As you can see in figure 6, the character for "east" conveys the idea of the sun rising in the east behind a tree. This character can be read as either *tō* or *higashi*. "East exit" is the straightforward translation of *higashi-guchi*.

Figure 7 shows the character for "south," which can be read either *minami* or *nan*. This comes from the depiction of plants growing inside a house or room with a sunny southern exposure. After a time, the character took on its present meaning of the direction itself. The Japanese for "south exit" is pronounced *minami-guchi*.

8. *kita* 北口 *kita-guchi*

9. *nishi* 西口 *nishi-guchi*

In figure 8 you can see the character for "north." This character depicts two men facing opposite directions, the backs of each supposedly being turned towards the sun. At least it would seem that

21

this is what one is asked to assume according to the old Chinese logic. The point is clear enough, however; when a person's back is towards the sun, he is usually headed in a northerly direction. This character can be read either *kita* or *hoku*. The former is used in the Japanese term for "north exit," which is pronounced *kita-guchi*.

Figure 9 gives the kanji for "west," which is generally read *nishi* or *sei*. There is a degree of uncertainty about the origin of this character. One theory has it that it represents a basket used by sake brewers in olden times. When they poured sake into the basket they always reckoned the direction of the flow as being a westerly one. Another, similar explanation of the origin is that in ancient times it was thought that everything, including sunlight, flowed towards the west. I might also add that the ancient Chinese believed that heaven was located in the west.

10. 中央口 *chūō-guchi*　　11. ⏀ → 中 *chūō*　12. 央 *ō*

The compound in figure 10 is read *chūō*, and means "central." The first character in this compound can be read either *chū* or *naka* (depending on the word in which it is used), and means "middle" or "central" (Fig. 11). In this case the former reading applies. The second kanji is pronounced *ō* and also has the meaning "central" (Fig. 12). As we go along, you will see that combining two characters with similar meanings to form a unique word is not an uncommon type of word formation.

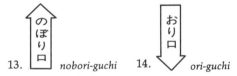

13. のぼり口 *nobori-guchi*　　14. おり口 *ori-guchi*

In addition to the five signs discussed above, other notices often seen at the station are shown in figures 13 and 14. These appear conspicuously on stairways, and they mean "going up" and "going down," respectively. In other words, the term read *nobori* in figure 13 means "go up," while the *ori* in figure 14 means "go down." When there is an entrance or exit at one end of the stairway where these signs are found, the character *-guchi* is included.

15. きっぷをはっきりお見せください。

Kippu o hakkiri omise kudasai.

At most stations you will see the sign in figure 15 above the ticket gate. Does it look familiar?

It reads, *Kippu o hakkiri omise kudasai*, which roughly translates as, "Please show your ticket clearly." By now you should be able to read all of the *hiragana* in this sentence. As you see, the only kanji is the character for *mi(seru)*, "to show," which is the same character as the verb *mi(ru)*, "to see."

16. ◁⊙ → ⊖ → 目 *me*   17. 𝄐 → 見 *mi(ru)*

You will probably appreciate this character more if you know that it depicts a big eye with legs, the legs representing a person (Figs. 16–17).

Figure 16 shows a person in the act of "seeing," a state I hope you are in right now. It is pronounced *me*. When you arrive at the station, be like the man in the character and look hard at all the signs. I hope you will soon recognize many of them. And don't forget, the ticket collector has big eyes too, so he will look very hard at your ticket! Make sure you have paid the right fare.

18. ◁ 左側通行   19. 右側通行 ▷

hidari gawa tsūkō   *migi gawa tsūkō*

In many of the stations you will see two other signs meaning Keep Left and Keep Right. The last three characters in both figures 18 and 19 are exactly the same, but since they are rather difficult we will leave them for now and concentrate on the first characters in each sign.

20. 左 *hidari*   21. 右 *migi*

The character in figure 20 is *hidari*, for "left," so it does not require great powers of deduction to figure out what the character in figure 21 means. They look very similar, so be sure and remember which is which.

The radical for "hand" appears as the upper left element of both characters. It is when we break the two down that we find the difference between them. The small I-shaped object on the lower right side of *hidari* is a measuring instrument or tool held in the left hand while working. You will recognize the lower right part of the character for *migi*, "right," as the character for mouth. It could be said that the ancient Chinese thought of the right hand in terms of its usefulness for putting food in the mouth. At any rate, having come this far you should now know your left from your right.

22. 山手線 *Yamanote Sen*

The busy *Yamanote Sen* ("Line"), linking twenty-nine stations, runs in a slightly irregular 34.5-km loop around the middle of the capital. About 550 trains are in daily operation on the Yamanote Sen, which shows more profit than any other line in the entire Japanese National Railways (JNR) system. The four busiest stations in Japan are all situated on this line. The first of these is Shinjuku Station, through which an average of 1,300,000 passengers pass on every ordinary working day. Ranking second, third and fourth, respectively, are Ikebukuro, Shibuya and Tokyo stations.

Although there are no mountains in central Tokyo, the word *Yamanote* (literally, "the hand of the mountain") was coined to distinguish the newer western part of the city, which is somewhat hilly and has a slightly higher altitude, from the Shitamachi area, which borders Tokyo Bay and is at or near sea level.

23. 〳〵 → ▲▲ → 山 *yama*

The first character in the combination for Yamanote Sen is pronounced *yama* (Fig. 23). This character is also the *san* of *Fuji-san*, "Mount Fuji." (*See* chapter 11.) It was originally drawn as three mountains. The illustration shows how it evolved to its present form. The second kanji is the one for "hand" and is pronounced *te*. The third one, meaning "line," is pronounced *sen*.

24. 外回り *soto mawari*   25. 外人 *gaijin*

The Yamanote Sen runs in two directions. These go by the designations "inner circle," *uchi mawari*, and "outer circle," *soto mawari*. Taking Shinjuku as the starting point, the inner line runs towards Shibuya and Shinagawa, while the outer line heads towards Ikebukuro and Ueno. You can remember which is which by telling yourself that foreigners have something in common with the outer line and housewives with the inner one. To understand this, take a good look at the first character for *soto mawari* (Fig. 24). This character can be pronounced *soto*, *hoka* or *gai*, and means "outside." A *gaijin*, literally speaking, is an "outside person" (Fig. 25). The second character means "person."

26. 内回り *uchi mawari*   27. 家内 *kanai*

The initial character in *uchi mawari* shows a person inside a house and means "inside" (Fig. 26). It is pronounced *uchi* or *nai*. The character for *ka*, "house," is the first one in figure 27. When these two characters are used together they are pronounced *kanai*, "wife." The ancient Chinese no doubt expected the wife to stay at home and raise kids. These days, urban wives are more apt to be found traveling on the Yamanote Sen, on their way to the big department stores and boutiques situated within walking distance of the main stations.

While on the train, a good way to pass the time may be by inspecting the colorful advertisements inserted in the curve of the ceiling or hanging over the aisles. On station platforms you can always be on the lookout for those directional signs devoid of English—of which there are examples galore!

28.   方 hō   方面 hōmen

One of the most common words seen on the platform is the one shown in figure 28. It is pronounced hōmen and translates as "direction." If you make a mental note about the lines in the first character—they point in all directions—you should have no trouble in recognizing it when you see it.

Now if you could read the place names you would know where the trains are going. This may appear to be a formidable task, but don't give up before you start—where there's a will there's a short-cut. Let's painlessly learn the names of the major stations on Tokyo's Yamanote Sen by concentrating on just one character in each compound.

29.   → 斩 → 新 shin   新宿 Shinjuku

First of all, let's take Shinjuku. The character on the left is pronounced shin or atara(shii), and means "new" or "fresh." Originally it was a picture of a tree and an ax; when you chop down a tree you expose new, fresh wood. The second kanji in the compound, pronounced shuku (-juku in some compounds) or yado, means "lodging" or "inn." (This is the shuku in shukuba.)

One of the liveliest night-life spots in Tokyo, Shinjuku dates from 1698. At that time, the first stop on the Kōshū Highway was Takaido, sixteen kilometers west of Nihonbashi. When a new shukuba was felt to be necessary, it took root near the present site of Shinjuku Station. Around 1868, the area had about fifty-nine inns and four hundred prostitutes.

30. 渋谷　*Shibuya*

Down the tracks a few stops from Shinjuku is Shibuya (Fig. 30). The simple character on the right pronounced *ya* or *tani*, means "valley" and originally depicted two mountains with water flowing between them. Geographically, Shibuya Station is located in a valley, which may explain why one subway terminal is on the third floor. In fact, there are a number of valleys, lying in such a way that groundwater collecting in low places took on a distinctive astringent taste identified in Japanese as *shibu(i)*, a word which also means "sober," "simple."

31. 品川　*Shinagawa*

Shinagawa is a striking combination of characters (Fig. 31). The first one is pronounced *shina* and means "goods." Its shape represents three mouths, suggestive of a large number of people, and where people congregate, there are lots of goods. Until the automobile age, Shinagawa was the starting point of one of the main routes leading from Tokyo to Kyoto, so many people and their possessions passed through this town. The second character in this compound, usually pronounced *kawa* (*-gawa* in some compounds), means "river."

32. 1 新宿　方面
　　　渋谷

Shinjuku
Shibuya　*hōmen*

33. 池袋　方面 2
　　上野

Ikebukuro
Ueno　*hōmen*

Now that you know how to distinguish whether a train is going in the direction of Shinjuku, Shibuya or Shinagawa, you should have no trouble reading the sign shown in figure 32. But how about the sign in figure 33? Don't worry, you'll soon be able to read this as well.

34. 東京 *Tōkyō*   35. 目黒 *Meguro*

Tōkyō, the largest city in Japan, literally means the "Eastern Capital." The station of the same name lies between the Imperial Palace to the west and Nihonbashi, the zero milestone from which all distances were once officially measured, to the east.

The first character is pronounced *higashi* or *tō*, and means "east" (Fig. 34). We saw it before in the compound *higashi-guchi*. You have also seen the eye-catching first character of Meguro, which is the character for "eye" and is pronounced *me*. If you remember, it formed the seeing part of the poor old chap with the bent body in *mi(ru)*, "to see". (*See* figure 16 above.) Together the characters with which Meguro is now written mean "black eye(s)" (Fig. 35). The place name itself goes back to the eighth century, but then it was written with different characters. For reasons unknown, the way of writing the name was changed, perhaps in the seventeenth century, and the kanji used today are ones found in the name of a temple located here and dedicated to the Buddhist deity Meguro Fudō.

36. ● → 上 → 上 *ue*   上野 *Ueno*

Ueno Park is certainly worth the trip, and after spending a few moments on the characters for Ueno you can soon be on your way. The character on the left is the symbol for "above," or "on top," and it is pronounced *ue*, *kami*, *jō* and so on (Fig. 36). It's former shape represented a mark above a line. The character on the right side of this compound is pronounced *no*, *ya*, and means "field," "plain." And in fact Ueno is geographically located on top of a knoll. It was once called Ueno Mountain or Ueno Forest.

37. 🐍 → 池 → 池 *ike*   池袋 *Ikebukuro*

Last but not least is Ikebukuro, after Shinjuku perhaps the busiest train station in the world. The left character is pronounced *ike* and means "pond." Look closely and you can see a snakelike creature slithering through the water (Fig. 37). The ancients, it seems, thought of the snake as being the king of the lake. The character on the right of this compound is pronounced *fukuro*, or *-bukuro* in some compounds, with the meanings "bag," "sack" or "pouch." The name Ikebukuro apparently stems from the presence of many round (*fukuro*-shaped) ponds in that area in times long past.

Armed with the ability to read these basic place names, you should be able to go anywhere on the Yamanote Sen. For a place name you can't read, ask somebody how many stops it is beyond a stop you do know. Listen carefully to all the conductor's announcements and watch the signs as they go by. (Don't cheat by reading the Romanized Japanese.) When wedged in a packed train, don't hesitate to ask any of the ten people standing next to you. What better time to practice your Japanese?

You say you're tired of the Yamanote Sen? Last night you could probably have ticked off more Yamanote Sen stops than the red-faced businessman slumped beside you. Now, expand your horizons by learning more about trains and the subway systems in the Tokyo metropolitan area.

38. 線 → 線 → 線 *sen*

First, you should learn the character *sen*, which means "line." This kanji generally follows the names of train and subway lines, as in Yamanote Sen. The left portion of this character means "thread" (depicting a bundle of thread), and the portion on the right means "fountain." Combined, these two radicals evoke the image of water from a fountain flowing in threadlike patterns or lines (Fig. 38).

39. 国 → 国 → 国 *koku*   国鉄線 *Kokutetsu Sen*

The people you have to thank for reminding you not to leave your umbrella on the train, for bringing Kyoto so much closer to Tokyo, for running the trains all night on New Year's Eve and many other things are the employees of the Japanese National

Railways.* To be sure you are under their meticulous care, look for the sign that resembles the one you see in figure 39, which says *Kokutetsu Sen*, or JNR Lines.

In order to recognize this sign all you really have to do is memorize the first character, which is pronounced *koku* or *kuni* and means "nation." As its original shape clearly indicated, *koku* depicts a king guarding a jewel within the boundary of his country. The second character is pronounced *tetsu* and means "iron" (short for iron rails).

40. 地下鉄線 *chikatetsu sen*　41. • → ﾗ → 下 *ka*

For a different look at Tokyo, venture underground where you see the words shown in figure 40. This sign indicates a subway line. The simplest character in this combination is the second one, pronounced *shita*, *ka* or *shimo*, and meaning "under," "below" or "lower." It used to be written simply as a mark drawn under a line (Fig. 41).

The third character in figure 40 is the *tetsu* in *Kokutetsu*. Here, too, it means "iron (rails)." The first character, *chi*, means "land," "ground" or "the surface of the earth." Altogether, we have a compound meaning "a train (that runs) underground."

42. 銀座線　43. 丸ノ内線　ｱｰ → 九 → 丸
Ginza Sen　*Marunouchi Sen*

44. 千代田線　45. 日比谷線　46. 有楽町線
Chiyoda Sen　*Hibiya Sen*　*Yurakuchō Sen*

The major subway lines in Tokyo are shown in figures 42 to 46.

*Under a government plan to reorganize the JNR beginning in the spring of 1987 the system will be divided into several companies, which will be placed under private management. This will result in some name changes, but the words and characters given in this book are common ones used in the everyday situations described and are unlikely to be replaced in the near future.

The Ginza Sen carries more people than any other subway line in the capital. Running generally east to west from Asakusa to Shibuya, it connects the main stations in the heart of Tokyo, including, of course, the cavernous Ginza Station. The Ginza Sen was the first subway to be built in Japan.

Again choosing one character to facilitate memorization, let's look carefully at the first kanji in this compound (Fig. 42). Pronounced *gin* and meaning "silver," it can be divided into left and right parts. Think of the left as representing a mountain containing metal. The right side originally provided the pronunciation, along with the meaning "white." Another word for "silver," using this kanji and preserving the Chinese way of thinking, is *shirogane*, literally, "white metal."

The second character in this compound, pronounced *za*, means "seat" or "to sit." In the Edo period (1603–1867) the mint for silver coin production was located in the Ginza. In other words, Ginza derived its name from being the "seat" for "silver."

The Marunouchi Sen boomerangs from Ikebukuro east through the center of Tokyo and then back west to Ogikubo. This shape is reflected in the first character, which is pronounced *maru* and means "circle" or "round" (Fig. 43). It evolved from a picture of a person wrapping his body around a valuable object to protect it. The second kanji was introduced as part of *uchi mawari*. Here too it is pronounced *uchi* and means "inside" or "interior." When the two characters are put together they roughly mean "inside the castle," signifying an important place. The Imperial Palace, which was once Edo Castle, is in the Marunouchi District. From the Meiji period until fairly recent times, this district has been notable for its concentration of leading financial and commercial interests.

47. のりば *noriba* 　48. のりかえ *norikae*

国鉄線のりば　　地下鉄線のりかえ
Kokutetsu Sen noriba　　*chikatetsu sen norikae*

Now that you know enough to get yourself pointed in the right direction when traveling, its time to give some attention to the fine print surrounding the characters you have learned.

Two important and ubiquitous words you'll see written in *hiragana* are *noriba* and *norikae* (Figs. 47–48). The former literally means "boarding area" and the latter "(place to) transfer."

49. こんどの電車は東京行き

Kondo no densha wa Tōkyō yuki.
This train is bound for Tokyo (Station).

50. 次の電車は中野行き

Tsugi no densha wa Nakano yuki.
The next train is bound for Nakano (Station).

Two other signs often seen above the platform are shown in figures 49 and 50.

51. 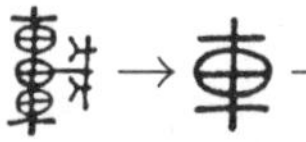 → 車 *sha*

52. 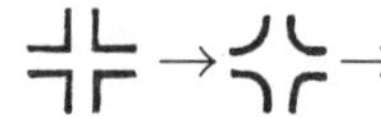 → 行 *yuki*

The word *densha,* "electric train," can easily be recognized if you just remember the character on the right of figure 51. This character is pronounced *sha* or *kuruma* and means "vehicle" or "wheel."

The character *yuki* basically means "to go" (Fig. 52). This character represents an intersection where vehicles and people stop and go. It can also be read *i(ku)* or *kō,* and is used interchangeably with *hōmen.* (*See* figure 28 above.) If a place name has *yuki* after it, it means that place is the train's last stop. Place names with *hōmen* after them are often just stops along the way.

53.

特急 *tokkyū* special express
急行 *kyūkō* express
快速 *kaisoku* fast (train)
準急 *junkyū* semiexpress
各駅停車(普通) *kaku eki teisha (futsū)* local train (ordinary)

How many times have you boarded an express train when you wanted to take a local and ended up way past your destination? This common and exasperating error can be avoided by reading the signs on the platform, or on the front, back or sides of the train (Fig. 53). Except for loop lines like the Yamanote Sen and subway lines generally, most government and private trains are classified and labeled according to their relative speediness in reaching their destinations.

Since some lines do not have the designations *kaisoku* for "fast (train)" and *junkyū* for "semiexpress," and since *tokkyū*, "special express," is not seen so often, let's concentrate on the other two.

54. 急行 *kyūkō*   55. 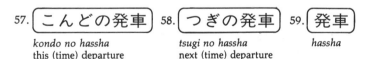 → 急 *kyū*

The character on the left in figure 54 is pronounced *kyū* or *iso(gu)* and means "hurry." Originally it was a picture of a person with a hand behind him, plus a heart (Fig. 55). In other words, we might say that when someone is chasing you and your heart is beating fast, you are in a hurry. Since the character *kō* was just introduced you should be able to read the compound in figure 54, *kyūkō*, literally "to go hurriedly," or in this case, "express."

56. 各駅停車 *kaku eki teisha*

I hope you remember the second character in *kaku eki teisha* (Fig. 56). After all, it is the first kanji discussed in this book. The whole phrase *kaku eki teisha* means "each-station-stop train," so a "local train." Alternatively, these slow trains are dubbed *futsū*, "ordinary (trains)." (Fig. 53, kanji in parenthesis.)

57. こんどの発車   58. つぎの発車   59. 発車

kondo no hassha　　*tsugi no hassha*　　*hassha*
this (time) departure　next (time) departure

Choosing between two identical trains on either side of the same platform, both heading in the same direction, presents a dilemma—two, in fact. Which one leaves first? And which one arrives at your destination first?

A look around you will reveal the answer; it is written well above the heads of the crowd on the departures sign (Figs. 57–58).

The first character of the compound *hassha* is, by itself, pronounced *hatsu* or, in some words, *-patsu*, and means "to leave" or "to start" (Fig. 59). The pronunciation comes from the sound of an arrow leaving a bow, and formerly this character included the character for "bow." Now, it has been simplified to the point where it cannot be analyzed by its parts to discover its original meaning. You will come across many characters which have been simplified over the years, making them easier to write, perhaps, but harder to remember.

60. 上り *nobo(ri)*   61. 下り *kuda(ri)*

Here's another choice you'll often have to make on train platforms, especially in the countryside.

You will recall that the characters in figures 60 and 61 mean "up" and "down," respectively. Since the seventeenth century, Tokyo has been a city to be looked up to politically, culturally and otherwise, so it is mentally envisioned as being on top of everything. This attitude still lingers in the distinction between *nobo(ri)* trains "going up" to the capital and *kuda(ri)* trains "going down." In practice, any train anywhere in Japan that goes even a short distance toward Tokyo, even if it never comes within hundreds of kilometers of the city, is called a *nobo(ri) densha*. (Just to confuse you, this may not always be the case. In Kyoto, for example, the words *nobo(ri)* and *kuda(ri)* are used to describe the actions of going towards or away from the Imperial Palace, no matter the means of travel.)

62. → ↳ → 手 *te* お手洗 *o-tearai*

63. 手洗い、御手洗 *tearai, o-tearai*   64. 便所 *benjo*

How many times have you seen the English word "toilet" written in bold letters over the entrance to a public restroom in Japan?

This is just an example of the consideration which the Japanese show to foreigners. The catch is that all the other signs leading up to the toilet are usually written in Japanese. When in need of a restroom in a public place, look for this sign, usually posted near the stairway.

Learn the compounds in figures 62–64, by all means! A few short minutes now could save you some very long minutes in the future. The first kanji in figure 62 you've already learned with the pronunciation *te* in Yamano*te* Sen, meaning "hand," and here it is indeed the picture of a hand. A second pronunciation is *shu* and additional meanings are "arm," "skill" and "control."

Literally, *o-tearai* means "hand-washing (place)," but actually it is a toilet. The place with facilities only for washing is called a *senmenjo*. (*See* chapter 10.)

In rural areas you may come across the word *benjo*, a much less refined term for "toilet" (Fig. 64). This is not a word heard in polite conversation.

65. 男 *otoko*   66. 女 *onna*

Knowing the characters for "men" and "women" is an absolute must and can save you some embarrassment. If you cannot read these the only sure way you will know which side of the public restroom or bathhouse to enter is to wait until someone happens along and walks in. But even this does not always mean you should follow him or her. Study figures 65 and 66. (Although recently there are many places that have a black or blue picture of a man and a red picture of a woman on the respective doors, there are still quite a few places, especially away from the big cities, where only the kanji for "man" and "woman" are used.)

67. 男 *otoko*   68. 女 *onna*

Also pronounced *dan*, the character for *otoko*, "man," evolved from a picture of a rice field plus a muscular arm standing for

35

chikara, "power," the meaning of the bottom part of this character (Fig. 67). The character for "woman," pronounced *onna* or *jo*, is a representation of a woman kneeling or sitting (Fig. 68).

69. 精算所 *seisanjo*

The reasons vary, but it happens to everyone at sometime or other. You've traveled farther than your ticket allows and you owe the railway company money. What to do? You can always try whisking nonchalantly through the ticket gate, but this seems to be one place where the Japanese are not intimidated by Westerners. The recommended course of action is to pay up. Whether it's JNR or a private line, the company has conveniently provided a window for that very purpose near the ticket gate. This is known as the *seisanjo*, "fare adjustment place" (Fig. 69).

You merely hand over your ticket at this window and the clerk will calculate how much you owe. After paying the difference, you are given a receipt to give to the ticket taker. Or, as you may have seen, at many train and subway stations, the fare adjustment is taken care of by the ticket taker himself when you give him your used ticket.

70. *sei*

To remember the meaning of this combination of characters, you need only memorize the first one. Pronounced *sei*, it means "clear" and comes from a picture of a rice plant on the left and a bud plus a well on the right (Fig. 70). Just as plants convey the feeling of clearness to the Japanese, *seisanjo* can be thought of as the place where money discrepancies are "cleared up." The second character in the compound, pronounced *san*, has the meaning "to calculate." And as you already know from the word *benjo*, the third character is *jo* (or *sho* or *tokoro*) and means "place."

2
Ticket Machines, Trains

If you have everything figured out ahead of time, you can buy the correct ticket without much trouble. In this and the next chapter, we will go into detail on how to use the different ticket vending machines you will need for everyday travel. Mostly, this means getting used to machines like the one in Fig. 3 below. Let's begin with those for *Kokutetsu*.

1. 新幹線　　　　山手線　　　　中央線
   Shinkan Sen　　*Yamanote Sen*　　*Chūō Sen*

Kokutetsu consists of all the train lines that have been operated by the national government. Seven of these are *Shinkan Sen*, the "New Trunk Lines," the *Yamanote Sen* and the *Chūō Sen* (Fig. 1). Actually, the JNR has four New Trunk Lines. The oldest of these (*Tokaidō Shinkan Sen*, 1964) runs from Tokyo to Osaka and its extension, the *San'yō Shinkan Sen*, goes on to Hakata in northern Kyushu. Unqualified references to "the *Shinkan Sen*" are invariably to these superexpress lines. The two other lines go northward from Tokyo—the *Jōetsu Shinkan Sen*, north and a bit to the west to Niigata on the Sea of Japan coast; and the *Tōhoku Shinkan Sen*, which extends as far as Morioka, Iwate Prefecture, in northern Honshu.

The *Chūō Sen* is another of Tokyo's major commuter lines. Actually, the commuter line is only the first section of the whole line, which runs deep into the Japan Alps.

2. 自動きっぷうりば　*jidō kippu uriba*

The words in figure 2 let you know you are close to a ticket machine. The first character in this phrase, *ji*, means "self." It is a drawing of a nose, and this undoubtedly has an intimate connection with the Japanese gesture of pointing at the nose to express the idea of "me."

The second character, *dō*, also pronounced *ugo(ku)*, consists of the characters "heavy," on the left, and "power," on the right. When force is applied to something heavy, it moves. And that is exactly what the meaning is here, "to move." Combine these two characters and you have, "self-moving," "automatic."

The word for ticket, *kippu*, has already come up once before. *Uriba*, "selling place," is made up of two words, a form of the verb *u(ru)*, "to sell," and *ba*, "place."

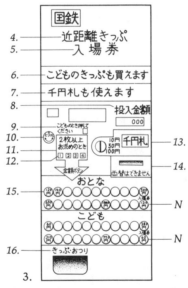

The tickets dispensed by automatic vending machines are primarily those for short distances and tickets for the station platform. In the machine shown in figure 3, the most expensive ticket is ¥1,540. Assuming this machine is located in Shibuya Station, this price ticket will take you as far as Miura, Kanagawa Prefecture, to the south, Tochigi to the north, Kimitsu in Chiba Prefecture to the east or Ōtsuki to the west. If you intended to travel beyond these points, you would have to buy your ticket at the *midori no mado-guchi*, the "green (ticket) window." (*See* chapter 4.)

4. 近距離きっぷ *kinkyori kippu*   5. 入場券 *nyūjōken*

The first kanji in figure 4 is pronounced *kin* or *chika(i)* and means "close." The second and third characters, *kyo* and *ri*, have similar meanings, "be distant" and "be separate," respectively. The meaning of *kinkyori kippu* is "short distance tickets."

In addition to train tickets you can also buy platform tickets from this machine. Pronounced *nyūjōken* (Fig. 5), these tickets allow you to go as far as any of the station platforms but not, of course, to board a train. In other words, they are useful for seeing a person off or meeting someone who needs assistance, such as a handicapped person.

As you have already learned, the first character in this combination, *nyū* (also pronounced *hai[ru]*) means "to enter" or "to go into." The second character, *jō*, *ba*, as you should recall, means "place." *Ken* means ticket. (*See* chapter 4.) The price of a *nyūjōken* is currently ¥120. Perhaps you will never have occasion to buy a platform ticket, but this term for a "ticket to enter a place" is worth remembering, as you will run into it here and there, at sightseeing places, for example, or observatories and so on.

Note the buttons identified by N on the right side in figure 3. To purchase *nyūjōken* you push these buttons.

6. こどものきっぷも買えます
Kodomo no kippu mo kaemasu.

This sign on a vending machine means that it has tickets for children. A child is eligible to use these tickets until graduation from elementary school at the age of twelve. The fare is half the adult fare. Note No. 9 in figure 3. You press the button labeled *kodomo*, "child," when buying a child's ticket. We'll discuss that in a moment.

7. 千円札も使えます
Sen'en satsu mo tsukaemasu.

The word for paper money in Japanese is *satsu*. If you don't have enough change, all you have to do is insert *sen'en satsu*, a "thousand-yen bill," into the machine. Then press the appropriate button, just as if you had used coins, and your change, along with your ticket, will come out at the bottom of the machine.

8. 投入金額 *tōnyū kingaku*

The amount deposited is displayed below the characters saying *tōnyū kingaku* (Fig. 8). The first character, *tō*, also pronounced *nage(ru)*, means "to throw." You have already met with the second character *nyū*. Together, these two characters mean "to throw into" or "to deposit." *Kin*, *kane*, means "money," and *gaku* added to a word means "amount." *Kingaku*, then, is the "amount of money" and *tōnyū kingaku* means the "amount of money deposited."

こどものとき押してください
Kodomo no toki oshite kudasai.

9.

| こども | *kodomo* |

The sentence in figure 9 says that when you want to buy a child's ticket, you should first push the button located here and having the word *kodomo* on it. Complete the process by pushing the button corresponding to the fare to your destination (Fig. 15 below).

10. とりけし *torikeshi*

Torikeshi means "cancel" (Fig. 10). This button is the round one on the left side in figure 3. To get back money you have deposited, just push this coin return button.

11. ２枚以上同じきっぷをお求めのときは枚数ボタンを
押してから金額ボタンを押してください。

It's possible to buy more than one ticket at a time. The rather long explanation of how to do this is given in figure 11. Since it would take us too far afield to explain everything, please take my word for it that is says, *"Nimai ijō onaji kippu o omotome no toki wa maisū botan o oshite kara kingaku botan o oshite kudasai."* Procedurally, this means, before pushing the button indicating the cost of a single ticket, press the button to tell the machine how many tickets you want.

12. **1 枚**   **2 枚**   **3 枚**   **4 枚**
ichi-mai   *ni-mai*   *san-mai*   *yon-mai*

The buttons offering a choice of the number of tickets allow you to buy up to four of the same priced tickets at one time. Arabic numerals are used here, so no problem. The kanji added to each numeral is pronounced *mai* and indicates that what is being counted is flat and, usually, thin—well, like a ticket (Fig. 12). The tickets will come out one after another, provided you have deposited enough money.

13. **10円**   **50円**   **100円**   **千円札**
jū en   *gojū en*   *hyaku en*   *sen'en satsu*

As indicated just below the word *tōnyū kingaku* (Fig. 8), coins—ten yen, up to fourteen at one time, fifty yen or one hundred yen—are inserted in the vertical slot at the center and one-thousand-yen bills go into the horizontal slot to the right of the coin slot (Fig. 13). If the machine accepts five-hundred-yen coins, there may be a separate slot for that purpose.

14. **両替はできません**   *Ryōgae wa dekimasen.*

Ryōgae wa dekimasen lets you know that the machine won't give change unless a ticket is purchased (Fig. 14). At large subway

41

stations there is usually a change machine next to ticket machines, so I have explained the meaning of *ryōgae* in chapter 3.

15. 金額ボタン　　　　　大人　　　こども
    kingaku botan　　　　*otona*　　*kodomo*

16. きっぷ・おつり
    kippu, otsuri

Now that you know what to expect from these friendly vending machines, it is time for a recap. After depositing your money, press the appropriate *kingaku botan* depending on your destination. *Otona*, "adult," tickets here range from ¥120 to ¥1,540. *Kodomo*, "children's" tickets are half the price of those for adults. As noted above, you have to first press the *kodomo* button at No. 9 to get a child's ticket. The *nyūjōken* button is located on the far right and is the last in the series of buttons. The tickets and your *otsuri*, "change," come out at the very bottom of the machine (Fig. 16).

In these examples I have used the current (as of late 1986) train fares for the *Kokutetsu* lines. It is likely that these fares will go up bit by bit, year by year. It will be interesting to see whether the machines will become ever more sophisticated and capable of handling ever larger sums of money.

3
Ticket Machines, Subways

Next, it's time to take a look at the ticket-vending machines for *chikatetsu sen*, the "subway lines." (The word *chikatetsu* is explained in chapter 1.)

There are two subway systems in Tokyo, the privately constructed Eidan Sen and the Toei Sen managed by the Tokyo metropolitan government. Since Eidan accounts for the greater percentage of the ten-line subway network in Tokyo, let's take a look at that first.

1. 営団線全線 *Eidan Sen Zensen*

The first character in figure 1, *ei, itona(mu)*, means "to operate" and the next one, *dan*, means a "group." Thus *eidan* refers to a group that operates something—here a subway system—or a "corporation." Although Eidan is privately owned, it is a corporation established for the benefit of the public. (The kanji for *sen* you already know.)

The last two characters pronounced *zensen* mean "all the lines." The whole phrase *Eidan Sen Zensen* says (redundantly), "all the lines of the Eidan Lines." What this means is that tickets for all Eidan lines are available. It appears at the top of these ticket machines (Fig. 2).

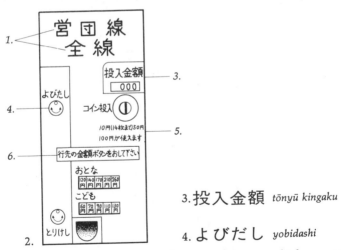

3. 投入金額 *tōnyū kingaku*

4. よびだし *yobidashi*

The expression in figure 3 is the same as the one which appears on JNR ticket machines.

If the machine is not working right (the ticket does not come out

43

or the change does not come back), push No. 4 button and a station attendant will be right there to help you. *Yobidashi* means "call," "summons."

5. 10円（14枚まで）50円、100円が使えます

Jū en (jūyon-mai made) gojū en hyaku en ga tsukaemasu.

On the right side of the machine, towards the middle, it says that you may deposit up to fourteen ten-yen coins along with fifty- and hundred-yen coins (Fig. 5). This particular machine does not accept five-hundred-yen coins.

6. 行先の金額ボタンをおして下さい

Yukisaki no kingaku botan o oshite kudasai.

Simply press the button for the appropriate ticket for your destination as indicated in figure 6. These fares range from ¥120 to ¥260. Just like the *Kokutetsu*, children's fares are half the adult fares. The *torikeshi*, "cancel," button is the same as that for the *Kokutetsu*,

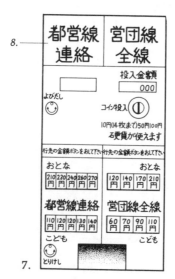

8. 都営線 *Toei Sen*

9. 都営線連絡 *Toei Sen renraku*

The other Tokyo subway system, the *Toei Sen*, is written as shown in figure 8.

When buying tickets, be careful not to confuse Eidan with Toei. This is possible because the two lines meet at such stations as Hibiya, Otemachi and Kasumigaseki and certain tickets for both lines can be purchased from the same machine. A careful look at the characters in figure 1 will prepare you for buying the right ticket. The Toei fares are a little more expensive than the Eidan fares, the former currently ranging from ¥130 to ¥340.

The character *to* in *Toei* can suggest simply "large town" (as opposed to countryside) as well as "capital," but here it has the latter meaning, as it does in *Tōkyō-to*. The *ei* is the same character as that in Eidan Sen and again means "to operate."

It is possible to transfer from an Eidan to a Toei line using a single ticket purchased at the point of origin. This will, in fact, save you money. To buy this type of ticket, you have to use a machine half of which is labeled *Toei Sen renraku* (Fig. 9). The buttons on these machines are neatly grouped in two blocks, those on the right for Eidan only tickets and those on the left for the transfer tickets.

Among machines of this type, there are also subway ticket machines that interface with JNR, machines that dispense transfer tickets between national and private railways, and so on.

When you don't know the total fare for your trip, consult the schematic map on which fares are indicated. These maps are posted over the machines. Station names appear only in kanji, but you can use the old trick of counting how many stops the station you want is from a kanji name you know.

This kanji saying you can purchase tickets for any Eidan line (Fig. 7, upper right) are explained under figure 2 in this chapter.

If you need change, look for a machine bearing the words

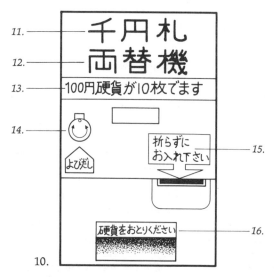

10.

sen'en satsu at the top (Figs. 10–11). *Satsu*, as noted before, means "paper money" or "bill." It should be easy to remember because paper is made of wood and the radical *ki*, for "tree," appears as the left side of this character.

11. 千円札 *sen'en satsu*   12. 両替機 *ryōgaeki*

The next word is *ryōgaeki* (Fig. 12). The exchange of a sum of money in one form for the same value in another form is called *ryōgae*. Used as a verb, the second character in this combination, *kae(ru)*, means "to change."

The *ryō* was a denomination of money in the Edo period. You've probably seen specimens of these beautiful, shiny gold coins, much larger and heavier than modern money, in museums. During the Edo period, one of these coins was worth slightly more than ¥33,000 in today's currency. Not surprisingly, ordinary people had few of these *ryō* and usually possessed only silver coins. The preservation of this word for "exchange" is an interesting example of vocabulary which has remained in use over a long period of time. (Another example of this is the word *sentō*. The reason public baths are called *sentō* is that the price of admission a few decades ago was one *sen*. The *sen*, 1/100th of a yen, is a denomination which has all but disappeared in these inflationary times. It is seldom encountered outside of financial institutions or commodity markets, where it is used to fine tune things like interest and dividend payments and currency and commodity quotations.)

The third character in the combination, *ki*, means "machine."

13. 100円硬貨が10枚でます *Hyaku en kōka ga jū-mai demasu.*

This sign tells you that you will receive your change in the form of one-hundred-yen coins. The *kō* in *kōka* means "hard" so the whole word means "hard money" or "coin."

14. よびだし   15. 折らずにお入れください
   yobidashi   *Orazu ni o-ire kudasai.*

Yobidashi has already been mentioned a couple of times (Fig. 14).

Figure 15 is a warning against folding a bill and a request that you smooth the money out flat before inserting it. As a further reminder, a picture of a hand doing just that appears over the slot for bills.

16. 硬貨をおとりください *Kōka o o-tori kudasai.*

After you have flattened and inserted a thousand-yen-bill, ten hundred-yen coins will drop from the lowest opening. This opening is labeled with the politely phrased expression, *Kōka o o-tori kudasai*, "Please take (your) coins" (Fig. 16).

4

Station Windows

To buy long distance train tickets, a commuter pass or coupon tickets, you will almost always have to go to a ticket window, although machines dispensing some of these are beginning to appear at some of the larger stations. Generally, you face a choice of more than one ticket window, even at smaller stations. To avoid wasting time at the wrong window, learn to recognize the following signs.

1. 定期券 *teikiken* 2. 回数券 *kaisūken*

Teikiken, a commuter pass (Fig. 1), is simple and convenient to use, but it can be difficult to obtain by oneself, since the application form is entirely in Japanese. Still, the famous Japanese kindness will probably bale you out. If you can find the right area, chances are someone will offer to help you fill out the right form.

3. 定 *tei*

4. 券 *ken*

The first character in this term is pronounced *tei* and means "be set," "be stipulated" (Fig. 3). And that is what a commuter pass is, a single pass-sized ticket good for a stipulated period and route of travel. This character evolved from a picture of a roof of a house and a foot stopped behind a line.

The second kanji in the compound is pronounced *ki* and means "time" or "period."

The third, pronounced *ken*, formerly depicted a sword being held by the hands of two different people, the idea being that a piece of wood cut with a sword and held between two men served as evidence of mutual agreement (Fig 4). It is like the legalistic idea that a ticket is a form of contract between seller and buyer.

5. → → 回 *kai*

Another way to save money is to buy a strip of coupon tickets at a somewhat discounted price. Learn to recognize the first character in figure 2. It is pronounced *kai* and means "to go around" and is added to numbers when counting "number of times" (Fig. 5). Coupon tickets are accordingly good for a certain number of rides at the rate, for example, of one per coupon. The second kanji in figure 2, which is pronounced *sū* or *kazu*, means "number."

6. *midori no madoguchi*

At the green ticket window you can purchase long distance tickets, reserved seat tickets, first class (so-called "green car") tickets, express and special express tickets, and others. Locating the green ticket window should be easy because, aside from the color itself, *midori* ("green") is written in hiragana and there is usually a sign above it depicting a person sitting comfortably in a very uncomfortable looking seat (Fig. 6).

7. → 手 → 扌
 → 旨 → 旨 → 指 *shi*

The first character in *shiteiken*, "reserved seat ticket," is pronounced *shi* or *yubi*, meaning "finger," or *sasu*, "to point." Some

49

say it is derived from a picture of a hand grabbing a spoon to put food in the mouth (Fig. 7). A reserved seat ticket might be thought of as the seat you decide on (*tei*, the second character) by pointing at it with your "finger" (*shi*). Actually, on Japanese trains—as opposed to planes—it is more often a matter of accepting the seat the computer chooses.

8. 国鉄指定券うりば *Kokutetsu shiteiken uriba*

The sign in figure 8 indicates that JNR reserved tickets are being sold at that particular counter.

The following are some of the common types of tickets (Fig. 9). Briefly, *gurīnken* is a first class ticket, *tokkyūken* is a "special express ticket," and *shindaiken* is a sleeping car ticket. *Shū yūken* is an excursion ticket sold at a discount and good for unlimited travel along specified routes within a certain time period.

9.
グリーン券 *gurīnken*   特急券 *tokkyūken*

寝台券 *shindaiken*   周遊券 *shū yūken*

Before leaving trains for other forms of transportation, I would like to explain how to recognize the information office, the lost and found office and the sign for "coin lockers," as well as give you a bit of information that I'm sure will come in handy sometime when you are standing waiting on the station platform.

10. 案内所 *annaijo*

The station, or any other, information office goes by the name of *annaijo* (Fig. 10). Here, you can get directions, train, plane and bus information and so on. Sometimes the attendants at *annaijo*, particularly in sightseeing or recreation areas, will phone and make reservations at local hotels or inns for you. In rural areas the information office is often situated in front of the station.

11. コインロッカー

koin rokkā

12. 忘れもの承り所

wasuremono uketamawarijo

Figures 11 and 12 are two other signs found in the station. The sign for "coin lockers," as they are called here (Fig. 11), points the way to rental lockers. Each locker has a slot to drop your coins into after putting your luggage inside. Then the key for that particular locker becomes yours, temporarily.

The lost and found office is on the train platform or somewhere else inside the station. It is not unusual for it to be inside the ticket gate. Look at the sign in figure 12. The first character, *wasu(reru)*, means "to forget." Here's an easy way to remember it: think of its original shape as that of a person hiding himself, for example, in the shadow of a wall, and add a heart to it. When a person's intentions (another meaning of the character for heart) disappear, as does his image when he steps into a shadow, he is in a state of absentmindedness.

13. こんどのでんしゃは　えびす　をでました

Kondo no densha wa Ebisu o demashita.

Once a beginning student of Japanese saw the above sign suddenly light up with "Ebisu," his destination, in big bright letters. Proud of his recently acquired ability to read Japanese, he very smugly stood under the sign and boarded the next train. As it turned out, the train was headed in the opposite direction. If he had read the whole message, he would have known that the information conveyed was that the train had just left the last station and would arrive soon. As is was, the hapless student boarded a train coming from Ebisu and not due to pass there again for about an hour (once around the Yamanote Sen).

5
Taxis

Now that you've mastered the art of hopping trains, it's time to move on to another subject. Let's take a look at taxicabs.

Don't let rumors of *kamikaze* cab drivers dissuade you from taking a taxi in Japan. The sobriquet was coined decades ago, and with a vast increase in the number of vehicles on the road, driving habits have changed quite a bit. Not only are Japanese cab drivers among the best in the world, but they routinely save foreigners and natives alike both time and headaches by finding obscure addresses. They can also complicate your social life and sleeping habits by allowing you to stay out long after the last train home.

1.

takushī noriba

2. 大型 *ōgata*

3. 中型 *chūgata*

4. 小型 *kogata*

The sign in figure 1 stands at the curb in front of hotels, train stations, airports and certain other places and, obviously enough, it is the way of writing "taxi stand" in Japanese. In some cities you will be given a choice of three different sizes of taxis: large, medium or small (Figs. 2–4). The larger the cab, of course, the higher the fare, but long-legged or luggage-laden Westerners are easily tempted to splurge on the bigger sedans.

5. → 大 *ō* 6. → 中 *chū* 7. → 小 *ko*

The first kanji in *ō-gata*, also pronounced *tai* and *dai*, etc., means "large" (Fig. 5). As can be seen from the illustration, it was derived from a picture of a man with arms and legs outstretched to give the feeling of "size" or "bigness," *ō(kisa)*.

The first character in *chū-gata* (Fig. 6) is the same as the first one in *chūō-guchi*. This kanji is simple enough. It shows a line drawn through the center of an object, thus depicting the ideas of "inside," "during" and "center."

Ko in figure 7, also pronounced *shō* or *chii(sai)*, comes from a sketch of three tiny dots and means "small." Until fairly recently, almost everything in Japan—TVs, refrigerators, trucks and whatnot—were *ko-gata* models.

Note that this use of *-gata* relating to size is only in reference to inanimate objects; for people, there are different words. Other pronunciations of this kanji are *kata* and *kei* and it has such meanings as "form," "model," "type" or "pattern."

People in and around Tokyo do not always have a choice of taxi sizes, but those who drive will want to remember this use of *-gata*. On toll roads and in parking garages and elsewhere, they will often see posted fees or road rules determined according to the size of a vehicle. (See *The Practical Guide to Japanese Signs, 2nd part: Making Life Easier*. Please note also that subsequent references to the companion volume to this one are given in the shorter form, simply "See *2nd Part*.")

8. 空車 *kūsha*   9. 回送 *kaisō*

A light inside the windshield of a taxi conveniently lets you know whether or not it is vacant.

If the cab is vacant, the light is red and when it gets close enough, you can see the word *kūsha* as red characters on a black background (Fig. 8). *Kūsha* literally means "empty car." Raise your hand and the taxi may stop for you.

Taxis which display no light or a green light are already occupied. Those having a sign saying *kaisō* (Fig. 9) over their vacancy indicators are on their way to a refueling stop, a bite to eat, the end of their shift or some other private destination.

10. 個人タクシー *kojin takushī*

A distinguishing phrase on some taxicabs is *kojin takushī*, which indicates that the driver is also the owner (Fig. 10). Many Japanese prefer these cabs to fleet-owned taxis, because they find the service to be better and, perhaps, the conversation more interesting.

For the unwary fresh arrival, there are a couple of things about taxis worth knowing: 1. Watch out for the car's left rear door, which is automatically opened and shut by the driver. He would appreciate it if you would let him control the door (rather than have you fight with the closing mechanism). 2. Pay the fare that appears on the meter. (Bargaining is definitely out, as it is generally throughout the country, although bargaining is practiced in a few situations like wholesale markets.) 3. As is true for the most part in Japan's service industries, no tipping is necessary. On the other hand, if the driver has been especially helpful—by giving a hand with awkward luggage, for example, or finding a particularly difficult address—it's all right to tip.

11. 目黒 へおねがいします *Meguro e onegaishimasu.* "I'd like to go to Meguro."

12. ここでおろして下さい *Koko de oroshite kudasai.* "Please let me off here."

If you are heading for an unfamiliar place, it might be a good idea to take along a piece of paper with the full address of your destination written on it in Japanese. Then, if you learn the two sentences in figures 11 and 12, you'll be all set—no more missing out on the party just to catch the last train!

6
Buses

There are not many long distance intercity through bus routes in Japan, because very extensive rail networks were built before bus travel became feasible. Of course, nowadays, anybody who wants to goes by plane. Chartered buses, on the other hand, are quite popular and in the city or a resort area, a bus may be the most convenient, the cheapest or the only way to get close to a certain locale.

The hardest part of bus travel is figuring out the signs found at bus stops. Place names naturally play a very significant role, and not only is their number legion, but the characters in names not infrequently have unique readings. A little persistence at the right time will pay off eventually.

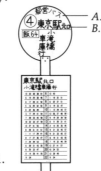

A.
B.

1.

The characters at the very top of this round sign identify the bus company—*Toei Basu*, in this case—and reassure you that this is indeed *teiryūjo*, a "bus stop." *Toei* is the same as in the subway *Toei Sen*, so the whole phase, *Toei Basu Teiryūjo*, means "Tokyo Metropolitan Bus Stop" (A in Fig. 1). Checking this part of the sign is not an idle exercise, since city and private bus lines may have stops quite close to each other.

B in figure 1 is the name of the bus stop. Below this in vertical writing are the route numbers and final destinations of the buses that stop here.

The rectangular sign at the bottom of figure 1 is a copy of the timetable for that route. The schedule for Sundays and holidays is written on one half (usually in red), under the heading *kyūjitsu*, "holiday(s)." (*See* figures 2 and 4.) The *heijitsu*, that is, "weekday," schedule (usually in black) takes up the other half of the timetable.

2. ☼ → ⊙ → ⊟ → 日 *jitsu*   3. ✍ → 日夂 → 時 *ji*

4. 🌳 → 休 *kyū*

The characters to be sure to learn now are the ones in figures 2, 3 and 4. The first, pronounced *jitsu*, *nichi*, *hi* or *bi* and meaning "sun" or "day," is, naturally enough, a picture of the "sun."

The next character, usually pronounced *ji* or *toki*, "o'clock" or "time," is a picture of the sun on the left and, on the right, a foot and a hand (Fig. 3). (Think of the movement of hands and feet as implying work. Nothing makes the time pass as quickly as being busy!) The right half has a long and complicated etymology. Its meaning of "work" became "government office," which then evolved to mean "temple." (*See* chapter 12.) This latter meaning comes from the association with Buddhist priests from India who, when traveling through China, were often put up in government offices.

The third character to remember is no sweat, so to speak. Pronounced *yasu(mu)* or *kyū*, it means "rest" or "vacation," and it is derived from a sketch of a person resting in the shade of a tree (Fig. 4).

A few final pointers on bus travel. The type of bus operation favored these days is *wan-man*, for "one-man," the second man, the bus conductor, having lost out to economics. So on Tokyo Metropolitan buses you deposit a set fare in the fare box when you board. On other buses, you may have to take a small slip of stiff paper (called *seiriken*) from a dispenser when boarding. The paper has a zone number on it, and when you are ready to get off, you check that number against the large electronic fare table at the front of the bus and deposit the *seiriken* with the appropriate amount of money into the fare box by the driver's seat.

Probably the easiest rule of thumb is this: if the front door is the one for boarding, it is a set-fare system. If you get on through the middle or rear door, the fare varies with the distance traveled. Coupon tickets and commuter passes are also available for bus travel.

By the way, don't neglect to push the buzzer as soon as the bus driver—or, more likely, a recorded voice—announces your stop. If nobody pushes the buzzer and nobody is waiting at the next stop, the driver will have no reason to do anything but sail right on by.

7

Airports

If you are planning a trip overseas, chances are very good that you will be taking off from *Shin Tōkyō Kokusai Kūkō*, the "New Tokyo International Airport" in Narita, Chiba Prefecture (Figs. 1 and 2). The exception to this are China Airline flights, which still come into and leave from the older airport at Haneda.

1. 新東京国際空港 *Shin Tōkyō Kokusai Kūkō*

2. 成田空港 *Narita Kūkō*　3. → 成 → 成 *na(ru)*

The *nari* in *Narita* can be thought of as depicting a hatchet and an overflowing container (Fig. 3). When a woodcutter cuts sufficient wood to fill his container, he considers it a good day's work. From this idea came the meaning *na(ru)*, "to become," "to accomplish."

The second character in this combination should be easy. The square boxes represent a larger area divided into *ta, den,* "rice fields," which is the meaning of this kanji. Growing rice was what the land was used for before the airport was built, and there are still lots of paddies in the countryside around the airport.

The next to last character in figures 1 and 2, *kū,* is also read *sora* and means "sky." The last, pronounced *kō* as well as *minato,* means "harbor." Together, these two characters add up to "sky harbor" or "airport." *Narita Kūkō* is the shorthand by which just about everyone refers to *Shin Tōkyō Kokusai Kūkō.*

4. 羽田 *Haneda*   5. → 羽 → 羽 *hane*

Before Narita, *Tōkyō Kokusai Kūkō* at Haneda served both international and domestic routes (Fig. 4). This airport, just a short journey by bus, taxi or monorail from central Tokyo, still handles domestic flights.

As you can see in figure 5, the first character in Haneda is a simple representation of the wings of a bird. Along with the second character it depicts a bird flying over rice fields—an interesting coincidence for the name of a place that was eventually to become an airport.

6. 航空会社 *kōkū-gaisha*

In Japanese, a company whose business is flying people ends its name with *kōkū-gaisha,* "airline company" (Fig. 6). In the case of the biggest of Japan's airlines, this is shortened to *Nihon Kōkū,* "Japan Air Lines." *Kaisha(-gaisha)* is the basic word for "company."

Since *kūkō* and *kōkū* are easy to confuse, it might be wise to pay special attention to the meaning of each character. The *kū* in both of these compounds is the same; as we have seen, it means "sky" or "air." The *kō* are completely different from each other. Taking a quick look at the *kō* in figure 6, we see a character that has evolved with the changing times. Originally this character stood for sea travel only, as is suggested by the left part—a boat. Now it is part of words like *kōkai suru*, "to sail," "to make (an ocean) crossing," and *kōkō suru*, "to navigate," "to cruise."

7. 飛行機 *hikōki*

The "airplane" you board at an airport is called *hikōki* (Fig. 7). The first character, *hi*, is also pronounced *to(bu)* and also means "to fly." The next character, *kō*, which has previously been introduced, means "to go." When we attach the last character, *ki* for "machine," we have a "machine that goes by flying."

8
Inns

One of the most interesting and stimulating activities in my own life is travel. No matter what the season of the year, travel in Japan can be enjoyable as well as educational. In the next few chapters I would like to introduce characters that have to do with temples and shrines, beautiful gardens, castles, Buddhist statues and the National Treasures you are sure to see on your journeys throughout Japan. At the same time, you can become familiar with vocabulary having to do with Japanese inns, Japanese baths, the Japan Travel Bureau, and a few of the more famous scenic spots in Japan.

1. 日本交通公社　2. 旅行会社　3. 観光案内所
Nihon Kōtsū Kōsha　　　*ryokō-gaisha*　　*kankō annaijo*

By now you should be able to reserve a train ticket. The next thing you will need to know about is reserving lodging. It is especially advisable to make reservations if you plan to go someplace during one of the holiday or other peak travel seasons. You can do so at one of three places: *Nihon Kōtsū Kōsha*, Japan Travel Bureau, (Fig. 1); *ryokō–gaisha*, a "travel agency," (Fig. 2); or *kankō annaijo*, a "tourist information office" (Fig. 3).

The Japan Travel Bureau (JTB) is Japan's biggest and busiest travel organization. Among other locations, it has dozens of offices in or near stations throughout the country. In addition to providing a myriad of free travel brochures, JTB can arrange all domestic and foreign transportation as well as lodging on your behalf. Usually an English-speaking employee is on hand.

The *Nihon* in *Nihon Kōtsū Kōsha* means "Japan." The third

character, *kō*, indicates the "coming and going" of people and things. *Tsū*, also pronounced *tō(ru)*, means "to go along" or "to pass through." Together, *kō* and *tsū* form the word for "transportation" or "traffic."

The next to last character in this company name, *kō*, can also be pronounced *ōyake*. The upper part represents a fence that has been opened so people can enter and leave freely, thus the meaning "public." It is the *kō* in *kōen*, "park" and *kōgai*, "pollution" (literally, "public damage").

4. *sha*

The last character, *sha*, consists of an altar on the left and a plant emerging from the earth, which by itself is the character for "earth," on the right (Fig. 4). Accordingly, this character means the place where the earth god, or another god, is worshipped, that is, a Shintō shrine. From the idea of people gathering together, this character took on the meaning of "association" or "company." *Kōsha* is a "public company," which is just the kind of company JTB is.

5. *ryo*

In figure 2 we had the word *ryokō*, meaning "trip" or "traveling." The first kanji, pronounced *ryo* or *tabi*, basically means "journey" (Fig. 5). It was originally a picture of people, who from early times traveled in a group, lined up behind a flag. Anyone who has seen a group of Japanese tourists trailing after a banner-waving tour leader will instantly appreciate how well this character has kept its appropriateness. The *kō* character in this combination is the one meaning "to go."

The third character in figure 2, *kai(-gai)* or *a(u)*, means "to meet." *Kaisha* (*-gaisha* at the end of a compound) indicates a privately owned "company." (Be careful not to confuse *kaisha* with *shakai*, "society," which is written with the same characters in reverse order.)

61

6. 🐦→觀→観 *kan*   7. 🔥→光→光 *kō*

Looking again at figure 3, we see a kanji consisting of a bird on the left and a large-eyed man on the right (Fig. 6). Think of this *kan* as meaning "to look around wisely and quickly," like a bird, in other words, "to view," "to observe," "to contemplate."

Kō, or *hika(ru)*, depicts in abbreviated form fire and a man (Fig. 7). When a man carries fire, say in the form of a torch, his surroundings become brighter; from this came the meaning of "shine" or "light." *Kankō* in the grand sense is traveling around viewing scenery or observing interesting things, or in plain English "sightseeing" or "touring."

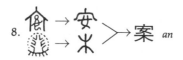

8.

The last word in figure 3, *annaijo*, "information office," was mentioned in connection with train stations.

The top half of the first kanji, *an*, is the *an* in *anshin*, "relief," "peace of mind." This meaning is contained in the depiction of a woman under a house roof. The bottom half is the radical *ki*, "tree." When these two halves are put together, you get the concept of peaceful contemplation beneath a tree (Fig. 8). Taking one more step we end up with a character meaning "plan" or "idea." Since the second character, *nai*, means "inside," the term as a whole can mean either "to invite" (someone to know your inside information) or, more simply, "to guide" or "to inform." In this word also, *jo* means "place."

9. 旅館 *ryokan*   10. 🏠→館→館 *kan*

If you stay at Western-style hotels in Japan only because you aren't sure how to make reservations at a Japanese inn, you'll soon be ready to try the alternative.

First, let's take a look at the characters for *ryokan*, "inn" (Fig. 9). The *ryo* is the *ryo* in *ryokō*, so we'll proceed directly to the second character, *kan* (Fig. 10).

The left part of *kan* is a character which means "eat," originally derived as a sketch of food placed in a vessel under a lid. The right side can be thought of as a picture of a dwelling, and together they suggest "food inside a house," in other words, an "inn" that also served meals. In keeping with this original meaning, the basic rate at a *ryokan* typically includes breakfast and often both supper and breakfast.

Many *ryokan* are steeped in history. In the old days, long before there were such things as cars or trains, most travelers had to walk to get anywhere. To house those weary people, *shōnin yado*, "merchants' inns," and *hatago*, traditional "inns," were built along main routes like the Tōkaidō, the Nakasendō and the Kōshū Highway. These were the predecessors of today's *ryokan*. In places like Takayama and Kiso there remain *ryokan* which were once the actual settings for many a famous samurai tale.

11. 民宿 *minshuku*   12. 宿 → 宿 → 宿 *shuku*

Although not as elegant as *ryokan*, the more inexpensive *minshuku* have become quite popular in recent years. *Minshuku* are generally managed by a single family as a seasonal or subsidiary business. For this reason, guests are pretty much left to look after themselves, and the atmosphere is generally much less formal than it is at a *ryokan*. Lodging at a *minshuku* can be likened to staying in a large private house where the rest of the family is in the other rooms. As a rule, meals, if available, are served in a common dining room, usually at a set time, and the guests must lay out and put away their own *futon* (bedding) and make their own tea.

Because the room rates at a *minshuku* are generally lower than at a *ryokan*, you cannot expect a great feast. Still, if the guest house is by the sea or in the mountains, you may be treated to a home-style meal of fresh fish or vegetables in season or some local delicacy that you would be hard put to find on more formal menus.

The necessary arrangements and reservations can be made at JTB offices or other travel agencies, or at regional *minshuku* centers or tourist information offices.

Min, the first character in *minshuku*, means "subjects," hence in a democracy, "ordinary people," "the general populace."

The second character is read *shuku(-juku)* or *yado* and consists of three elements (Fig. 12). You have already met with the radicals on the top and the left of this character; they mean "roof" and "person," respectively. The element forming the lower right part is the word for *hyaku*, "hundred." This leads to the idea of *yado*, a place where a hundred (or more) people stay beneath the same roof.

As you may have noticed already, the *shuku* of *minshuku* is the *-juku* of Shinjuku. Shinjuku has long been a popular place for travelers, and because of its location on the Kōshū Highway, this area was dotted with inns for the throngs just arriving in or getting ready to leave the capital. The literal meaning of Shinjuku is "New Inns."

9
One Night, Two Meals

Let's study some words and phrases which will be among the most useful when you actually go to a travel agency to make reservations for a *ryokan* or *minshuku*. As noted in the last chapter, breakfast and dinner are customarily figured in with the price of a night's lodging at *ryokan*. This is not always true of *minshuku*, so it is best to check beforehand.

1. 一泊二食付き *ippaku nishoku tsuki*

This arrangement is known as *ippaku nishoku tsuki* (Fig. 1). *Ippaku* means "one night's lodging." The first character, *ichi*, "one," here has an abbreviated pronunciation. The second character is pronounced *haku(-paku)* or *toma(ru)*. As you can see, this character has two basic components: on the left is a reduced form of the radical for "water" or "river"; the component on the right by itself means *shiro*, "white." Just as white to the Japanese evokes the image of thinness or scarcity, a white river is equated with a shallow river. When a boat reaches the shallow part of a river, it is time to stop, and this is the idea we associate with this character meaning "to stop (for the night)" or "to put up at."

The third and fourth characters in this phrase mean "two meals." *Ni* means "two." *Shoku*, "meal," is also pronounced *ta(beru)*, meaning "to eat."

2. 付 *tsuki*

The last character in figure 1 is pronounced *tsu(ki)*, *tsu(ke)*, *tsu(ku)* or *fu*. If you study this character, you will find that the left side stands for the figure of a man and the right side signifies a hand holding an object (Fig. 2). The idea is of one person handing an object to another. This explains one meaning, "to give." The right side also suggests a hand attaching something to a person's back, and from this we have another meaning, "to attach," "to affix" and, by extension, to be included.

3. 宿泊料金 *shukuhaku ryōkin*

It is time again to talk about money, specifically the money paid to stay at a *ryokan* or *minshuku*. This goes by the name of *shukuhaku ryōkin* (Fig. 3). Neither of the first two characters is new to you. *Shuku*, "lodging," is the same as in *minshuku* and *haku*, "stay," is the same as in *ippaku*.

That brings us to *ryō,* which means "fee," "rate" or "material." And finally we come to *kin,* "money," "gold," as an independent character. Together, these two kanji make up the word *ryōkin,* meaning "fee," "rate," "fare" and so on.

The payment of *shukuhaku ryōkin* formally completes the reservation process. As proof of payment, the travel agent will issue a *shukuhakuken,* and this becomes your reservation certificate to be handed over when you check in.

4. 予約 *yoyaku*

The actual word for reservation, no doubt printed somewhere on the *ken,* is *yoyaku,* and it literally means "to agree," *yaku,* "in advance," *yo* (Fig. 4).

Think of *yo* as representing the shapes of a number of rare objects. Before one presents a rare object to another person, he must first consider his action. From the idea of premeditation, we have the idea of any action taken in advance.

The second character, *yaku,* depicts a skein of thread and, supposedly, a person embracing an object. If we accept the idea of gathering up various things and tying them together, we can easily derive the meaning of this kanji: "promise," "conclusion."

Below are some alternatives to *ippaku nishoku.*

5. 二泊四食 *nihaku yonshoku*   6. 三泊六食 *sanpaku rokushoku*

10
Baths

In inns, stations, older houses and many other places, you'll come across sinks—metal, stone or cement, large or small, with one to half a dozen or more taps. Obviously, these places are for washing and they most often go by the name of *senmenjo* (Fig. 1).

1. 洗面所 *senmenjo* 2. お手洗 *o-tearai*

3. 洗 → 洗 → 洗 *sen*

Don't be one of the people who confuse this word with *o-tearai*, "toilet," just because both contain the character *sen*, *ara(u)*, "to wash" (Fig. 3). (*O-tearai* was given in chapter 1 but is repeated here so you can have the two words side by side for comparison.)

The left side of this *sen* character clearly represents the flow of water, and the feet at the bottom of the right side can be thought of as being beneath grass. Taken altogether, we can imagine a man walking across a grassy riverbank to clean his feet in the river.

The second character is read *men* or *omote*. Some say the center-most part shows the shape of a face, around which are lines drawn to accentuate and delineate the space occupied by the face. Others say the whole character is the face and the center part is the nose. Either way, this character means "face," "surface," or "(out)side." You may remember this character from the signs about train destinations, in the word *hōmen*, "direction."

By the way, although you'll never hear it in casual conversation, *senmen* is a word in its own right, meaning, needless to say, "washing the face."

For the third character in *senmenjo* you have, once again, the pronunciations *jo*, *sho* and *tokoro* and the meaning "place." Like many kanji compounds, this is probably best translated by a phrase, a "place where one washes one's face," since the literal "face-washing place" is awkward and both "lavatory" (in its everyday meaning) and "washroom" imply toilet, which *senmenjo* does not.

As you have already learned one sign for "restroom," we won't go into it again. Although most *ryokan* have Western-style restrooms as well as Japanese style, many *minshuku* still have only Japanese-style facilities. If this is likely to be a problem for you, feel free to check before making reservations.

Next, we come to the question of tipping. Since tax and service charges are generally included in the room rate at *ryokan* (some *ryokan* list them separately on the bill), there is no obligation to tip for room service. However, as with taxis, it is not out of place to offer a small tip if you have received special service or notable kindness from the proprietor or servants. I recommend that you use your own judgment according to the circumstances. At *minshuku* you pay neither service charges nor tips. As noted earlier, self-service is the rule.

I hope you'll try your hardest to speak Japanese to the *ryokan* staff and will have many pleasurable journeys to remember for years to come.

After reaching your *ryokan* and taking a short rest, you may very well decide to relax with a bath before dinner. In the more expensive *ryokan* each room is equipped with bath, shower and toilet, but in the medium range the bath is almost always shared by all the guests. Here, I would like to introduce the signs that will lead you to the bath and keep you on the right path.

4. 浴室 *yoku shitsu*   5. 沿 → 沿 → 浴 *yoku*

The most common sign is *yoku shitsu*, literally "to bathe" plus "room" (Fig. 4). Immediately after this usually comes the character for *otoko*, "man" or *onna*, "woman." Please be sure you enter the appropriate room.

The first character is read *yoku* or *abi(ru)* (Fig. 5). The left radical in this character is the one signifying "running water," and on the right is the opening from which water flows. Because in olden days people bathed in water flowing out of springs in the ground, the character has the meaning "to bathe."

In the second character, *shitsu*, "room," you will recognize the upper part as being the roof of a house. The character beneath it has the meaning "to attain" and "utmost." In combination these two components refer to the innermost room, where people can meet or sleep safely without fear of disturbance. In a Japanese castle, this would probably be a room right in the middle, well away from the outer walls.

6. 大浴場 *daiyokujō* 7. 千人風呂 *sennin buro*

Ryokan at hot spring resorts usually feature enormous baths. About the size of the public baths found in Tokyo, they are often decorated with rocks or plants to create a pleasing, natural atmosphere. The owners do not hesitate to boast of such attractions in their advertisements, and you will often see baths proudly on display in brochures and other ad media. They even get called special names: *daiyokujō*, for example, or to really emphasize their spaciousness, *sennin buro*, "a bath (big enough) for a thousand people" (Figs. 6–7).

Soaking in a hot bath the size of a swimming pool is surely one of life's sybaritic experiences. And at a hot spring the water is constantly replenished with bubbling abandon.

The first character in figure 6, pronounced *tai*, *dai*, *ō* and *ō(kii)*, was introduced in chapter 5. As you will recall, it means "large" or "big."

The third character, *ba*, meaning "place," is added to quite a number of words, and it may also, as here, have the pronunciation *jō*. *Daiyokujō* is a "large bathing place," much larger than any *yoku shitsu*.

8. 家族風呂 *kazoku buro*

When you and your family want to bathe together, you should ask for *kazoku buro*, the "family bath" (Fig. 8). If the place you are staying has one, it will be about the size of a bath in a private home and will probably have a small anteroom for dressing and a lock for privacy.

The *ka* character of *kazoku buro* may also be pronounced *ie* or *ya* or, unofficially, *uchi*. This kanji was briefly mentioned in chapter 1 as part of the word *kanai*, "wife." The upper part represents a house roof and the lower the shape of a pig (Fig. 9). The ostensible reason for the pig is that one or more of these animals were usually kept inside the ancient Chinese house.

In almost all cases the second character is read *zoku* (Fig. 10). The left side and upper right element represent a flag. The lower right part represents three arrows. From three arrows lined up below a flag we can derive the meanings "troop," "comrades" or "family." *Zoku* and *kazoku* have the last meaning in common.

Going on to the final kanji in this compound, it is read *fū*, *fu* (*-bu*) or *kaze* and combines the figures of a ship's sail and an insect (some say snake). When the wind blows a ship's sails flutter; the blowing of the wind also gives birth to insects, or at least influences their behavior. Putting these two concepts together we not only have the meaning of "wind," but also "style," "form," "appearance." Although it is not clear why the character "wind" is used in making the word for "bath" (*furo*), it seems likely it was included only for its pronunciation. The last character, pronounced *ro*, is also used solely for its phonetic value.

11. 露天風呂 *roten buro*

The uniqueness of one type of natural hot spring bath quite popular in Japan is evident in its very name, *roten buro*, which means "outdoor bath" (Fig. 11). Most *roten buro* are surrounded by a wooden fence for the sake of privacy, but there are many left in plain view of anyone who happens to be nearby. For this reason women usually prefer to wait for the cover of night to slip into the warm comfort of a *roten buro*.

11
Natural Features

Now that you are nicely settled in at your *ryokan* or *minshuku*, you can think about some characters to make your travels in Japan more informative and interesting. We'll start with three simple, common characters and go on from there.

1. ∧∧ → ▲▲▲ → 山 *yama*   2. 富士山 *Fuji-san*

Since more than two thirds of the land area of Japan is mountainous, it is unlikely that you will go far before seeing the character in Fig. 1.

I introduced this kanji, pronounced *yama*, *san* or *-zan*, in the word Yamanote Sen. Note that when it is part of the name of a mountain, as in *Fuji-san*, "Mount Fuji" (Fig. 2), or *Aso-san*, "Mount Aso," the reading is very often *san*, not *yama*.

3. ∫∫∫ → /// → 川 *kawa*   4. 🌿 → 朩 → 木 *ki*

5. 🌿🌿 → 朿 → 森 *mori*

Figure 3 shows another easy character, the one meaning "river," pronounced *kawa(-gawa)* or *sen*.

The character for *ki*, "tree," "wood," needs no explanation, as its shape is self-explanatory (Fig. 4). Three of these characters in the right pattern yield another word, pronounced *mori* and meaning "forest" or "woods" (Fig. 5).

6. 国立公園 *kokuritsu kōen*   7. → → 立 *ritsu*

One or more of these characters are likely to turn up in printed information about the twenty-eight "national parks" of Japan, which are called *kokuritsu kōen* (Fig. 6).

You should know half the characters in this compound. The first, *koku*, "country," was introduced in *Kokutetsu*, "national railways." The third, *kō*, "public," was seen in *kōtsū kōsha* (JTB).

That leaves the second and the fourth. The second, pronounced *ritsu* in this case, comes from a picture of a man standing on the ground and looking straight ahead (Fig. 7). This character is the common verb *ta(tsu)*, "to stand," but here it has the meaning "to be established." Obviously, anything designated as *kokuritsu* has been "established by the nation."

This expression ends with the character *en*, *sono*, meaning either a large enclosed piece of land or a "garden." Look carefully at how it is written. You will notice that, like the character for "nation," there is a square on the outside. A character enclosed by a square generally designates a place surrounded by a fence. Unfortunately, this is truer today than it was when the character came into being; more and more parks and gardens in Japan are ending up behind barriers or fences.

8. 温泉 *onsen*

Being volcanic, Japan is a country well endowed with lakes and "hot springs." The term for the latter is *onsen* and they are a favorite with young and old alike (Fig 8). Not only are hot springs said to be good for diseases—intestinal, skin, nervous, rheumatic or what have you—but they are also supposed to help women who have difficulty giving birth. There are numerous kinds of hot springs, some containing sulphur or phosphorus, others salts or minerals like iron. Each has its own characteristic odor and color.

Hot springs, said to have been discovered during the age of the gods, have been valued in Japan since the dawn of history. Mention of them is made in Japan's oldest collection of poetry, the

Manyōshū (eighth century), and in the first historical record, *Nihon Shoki* (eighth century). Some of the most frequently visited hot springs are located in Izu (convenient to Tokyo), Noboribetsu in Hokkaido, and Beppu in Kyushu.

9. 氵🅻 → 湿 → 温 *on*   10. 🅵 → 🅵 → 泉 *sen*

The first character in this compound is read *on* or *atata(kai)*, and, according to one theory, it evolved from a picture of a small dish containing an object placed inside a larger dish (Fig. 9). Since the purpose of such an arrangement is to prevent heat from escaping, the character has the meaning of "warmth," "heat." An interesting thing about this character is that, although it has the water radical, none of its meanings are directly related to water or rivers.

The second character in *onsen* also has the pronunciation *izumi*. The shape of this kanji comes from water flowing out of a deep rocky hole, hence the direct meaning "fountainhead" or "spring" (Fig. 10). Combined, the two characters indicate the source of hot water.

11. 🅻 → 氵湖 → 湖 *ko*

Among the famous lakes in Japan are Lake Biwa, the largest; Lake Chūzenji in Nikko National Park, a mountain lake twelve hundred meters above sea level; and five lakes created ages ago when lava flowing from Mount Fuji damned mountain valleys, among which Lake Yamanaka and Lake Kawaguchi are especially well known. When used with a name, the character for "lake" is pronounced *ko*, as in *Biwa-ko*, *Chūzenji-ko*, *Yamanaka-ko*, etc. Independently the word for "lake" is pronounced *mizuumi* (Fig. 11).

Here again the left side is the radical for water. The two elements on the right suggest the reflection of the moon in a large pond filled with tall grasses. Logically enough, this gives the meaning "big pond" or "lake."

12. 水🐚 → 渁 → 海 *kai*

While we are on the subject of water, let's take a deeper look.

Geographically speaking, Japan is long and narrow, so it doesn't take more than a few hours to reach the seacoast from any point in the country. For many Japanese, *umi*, the sea, is very much an integral part of life (Fig. 12).

Along with the radical for "water" on the left, this character has the seemingly odd combination of sprouting grass (top) and mother (lower right). The story woven around this is that, in the same way mother grass produces abundant young grass, the waters of a river flow and spread out, forming the sea. Well, that's how the ancients saw it anyway. When this character becomes part of a name, it is pronounced *kai*, as in *Nihon Kai*, "Sea of Japan," and *Setonai Kai*. For some reason, the latter has long been known in English as the "Inland Sea." This is a misnomer. With both ends being naturally and completely open to the Pacific Ocean, it can hardly qualify as "inland." A translation of the Japanese reveals the real situation: "sea within channels."

13. 海岸 *kaigan*   14. 辰 → 岸 → 岸 *gan*

Sadly, much of the once-beautiful seas around Japan are now polluted, but there are still a number of *kaigan*, "seacoasts," worth visiting (Fig. 13). Centuries of volcanic activity and earthquakes have created breathtaking seascapes on the Izu and Noto peninsulas, and there are many other shorelines justly famous for their beauty even now.

As you already know the first character of this word, let's go on to the second one, pronounced *gan* or *kishi* (Fig. 14). The top part is a mountain, which in countless landslides has been sending debris down to meet the water. The lower part can be thought of as crumbling cliffs (Fig. 3). The meaning attached to this is "edge of the water."

15. 浜 *hama*

Closely related to the word *kaigan* is *hama*, implying a flat sandy area by the sea, that is, a "beach" (Fig. 15). Students tend to get confused over the difference between *kaigan* and *hama*. Think of the former as the geographical term having the broader meaning of areas where the sea meets the land, hence "coast." *Hama* is more closely associated with people. You have a choice: imagine tens of thousands of people carpeting the beaches at the height of summer, or think of *hama*'s other meaning, "fishing village."

16.  *shima*

We had a word (*on*) with the water radical whose meanings are rarely related to water. Now let's consider something that exists only in relation to water, but written with a character not having the water radical: *shima(-jima)*, *tō*, "island" (Fig. 16). With the total number of islands of various shapes and sizes in the Japanese archipelagos being no less than 3,922, this kanji is one you will encounter often.

The idea of this character is fairly simple, for it is nearly identical to the one for "bird," with "mountain" included at the bottom in place of four dotlike strokes. (*See* chapter 19.) The character is very like the archipelago itself; mountains pushing up from the seabed make islands, where birds flying across the sea may stop to rest.

12
Shintō and Buddhism

If you travel to an area of historical or cultural interest in Japan, you are bound to come across a shrine or a temple. Let's take a look at shrines first and then temples.

1. 神道 *Shintō* 2. → → 神 *shin*

It is not known for sure exactly when it originated, but *Shintō*, the native religion of Japan, seems to have come down to us from the mythological ages. In the beginning it was directly related to the worship of the sun goddess, Amaterasu Ōmikami. Over the centuries, it was influenced by the more philosophical Confucianism, Taoism and Buddhism and underwent many transformations. Religion and state are clearly separated in the present age, although there have been times in Japan's history when Shintō and the national polity were tightly interwoven.

The first character in figure 1, *shin*, also has the readings *jin* and *kami*. The left side of this kanji depicts an altar, the right side three thunderbolts (Fig. 2). The Chinese of antiquity believed thunder was a manifestation of a heavenly "god," which is the meaning of this character. Later on, all sorts of awe-inspiring things were revered as gods. Perhaps you'd be interested to know that the sun, mountains, stars and a myriad of other manifestations of nature were all once gods in the minds of the Japanese.

The usual pronunciations of the second character in figure 1 are *dō* and *michi* and the usual meanings "road" or "way." Like the comparable English terms, its meanings span both the concrete, as in a "highway" for vehicles, and, as here, the abstract, a virtuous or religious "way" or "path."

3. 神社 *jinja*   4. 神宮 *jingū*

Jinja, a Japanese "shrine" is a place for worshipping the Shintō gods (Figs. 3–4). Distinguished heroes are enshrined in famous places like Nogi Shrine in Tokyo and Yasaka Shrine in Kyoto, while local deities are worshipped at shrines large and small throughout the land. You may have seen processions of portable shrines being carried through the streets at festival time. These honor the local deities who look after the local people, who joyously do the carrying.

The character for "god" has the pronunciation *jin* in both figures 3 and 4. The second kanji in figure 3, pronounced *ja*, you should recall as the *sha* of *kaisha*. As noted in chapter 8, the original meaning of this character was a "place to honor the gods."

Figure 4 shows the combination *jingū*, another word which translates into English as "shrine."

The reason there are two words for "shrine" is that *jingū* designates a place of worship dedicated to a particularly noteworthy emperor or an imperial ancestor. In English it sometimes becomes "Grand Shrine." Some examples are Meiji Jingū, dedicated to the Meiji Emperor; Ise Jingū, erected and preserved to honor the goddess Amaterasu; and Heian Jingū in Kyoto, which enshrines the emperor who over a thousand years ago created that former capital.

5. *gū*

The character for *gū* may also be read *kyū or miya* and originally depicted a place filled with many square rooms (Fig. 5). It can be a place to honor the gods or an imperial residence.

Shintō priests are either *gūji* ("chief priest") or *kannushi*. If you have occasion to address one, the honorific to use is *gūji-san* or *kannushi-san*.

In contrast to the indigenous Shintō, *Bukkyō*, "Buddhism" (Fig. 6), came from India, where it originated as the shared beliefs of the followers of Shakyamuni Buddha, and was formalized in Japan in the mid sixth century. Then in 594 the regent Shōtoku Taishi promulgated an imperial edict to support and encourage the recognition of the Three Treasures: the Buddha, the Law (Dharma) and the Priesthood (Samgha). He established many temples, the most famous of which is probably Hōryūji in Nara. Dating from 607 it has long since become the oldest wooden structure in the world.

6. 仏教 *Bukkyō*   7. 彿 → 沠 → 仏 *Butsu*

As an independent character, the first element in *Bukkyō* is pronounced *Butsu* or *Hotoke*, "the Buddha" (Fig 7). The left side of this kanji is the radical *nin*, "person." The right seems to represent running water and steam and has the meaning "to disappear." This accords with the Buddhist concept that to reach enlightenment a man must rid himself of all egotistic thoughts so the self will disappear.

The second character, *kyō*, *oshie(ru)*, is said to depict a busy father. While sternly lecturing his son, he is beating him with a stick. The idea is "to teach." Another way of expressing the meaning of this compound is "The Teachings of the Buddha."

8. ⩜ → 步 → 寺 *tera*

As a convenient way of differentiating them from Shintō shrines, Buddhist places of worship in Japan are called "temples." In Japanese they are *tera* or, as a suffix, *-dera* or *ji* (Fig. 8). Look very closely and you will see a hand and foot. This kanji originally meant a government office, where many people were always bustling about, moving their hands and feet. The people in question happened to be Buddhist priests, so this character came to mean "temple."

Buddhist priests are referred to as *sō* or *sōryo*, but when addressing one directly the term *obōsan* is preferred.

9. 𥔵 → 示單 → 禅 *Zen*

Before leaving Buddhism, we should mention Zen. Transmitted from China as early as the eighth century, Zen became firmly established in Japan from the late twelfth century, and today it is to the outside world a symbol of Japanese culture.

The left part of *Zen* represents an altar (Fig. 9). The right side is a weapon split into two from its tip. This signifies that the two functions of a weapon, defense and offense, are one. Perhaps this has something to do with the ultimate objective. In Zen, enlightenment is attained through meditation, and once attained the self becomes indistinguishable from the substance of the universe. There are no longer any discriminations of any kind, nor any opposites like defense and offense.

13
Statue and Garden

The main halls of temples you will visit almost always contain Buddhist statues. Some halls have hundreds. A city especially noted as a treasury of beautiful Buddhist images is Nara, and it is there, at the Tōdaiji, that you can view the largest Buddhist statue in Japan, *Daibutsu*, "the Great Buddha."

Because the city was briefly the capital, Nara is the name of a historical period (710–94) as well as a city. It was then that these great works of art were made by imperial request, for it was thought that erecting these images would drive away plagues and other misfortunes.

1. 仏像 *Butsuzō*   2. 猩 → 像 → 像 *zō*

How do you suppose the word *Butsuzō*, "Buddhist image," was derived (Fig. 1)? Don't laugh, but it brings together on the left side a human being and on the right side an elephant (Fig. 2). *Zō*, "elephants," being huge animals, their presence is easy to discern, even at a distance. From this fact, this character took on the meaning *shō*, "figure," "shape" and, eventually, "image." Add "man" to this kanji and you have "image of man," hence "picture," "statue." This character has only the one reading, *zō*.

3. 国宝 *Kokuhō*   4. 🏠 → 宝 → 宝 *hō*

After inspecting all the Buddhist statues in Japan, the government has designated those that are outstanding aesthetically or historically as *Kokuhō*, "National Treasures" (Fig. 3). There is usually a small plaque informing the viewer of this fact. Other National Treasures are buildings, art and craft objects, scrolls and the like. The Golden Pavilion and Nijo Castle, both in Kyoto, and Tōshōgū Shrine in Nikko are three of many National Treasures.

Individuals are singled out for this honor when they have proven themselves supreme masters of their calling, which may be a performing rather than a representational art. He or she is then given the title *Ningen Kokuhō*, Living National Treasure. (The literal translation is "Human National Treasure," since *ningen* means "human being.")

Besides "treasure," the *hō* character in *Kokuhō* has the meaning "jewel," the idea being that of a jewel being stored inside a house (Fig. 4).

5. 拝観料 *haikanryō*   6. 🙏 → 拝 → 拝 *hai*

The next time you visit a temple or a shrine housing a National Treasure, you might like to take note of the sign with the term *haikanryō* written on it (Fig. 5). It will be followed by figures giving the "admission fees" for adults and children.

Haikan combines the two verbs *hai(suru)*, "to worship," and *kan(zuru)*, "to look at." Both *kan* and *ryō* were seen before, one in *kankō*, the other in *ryōkin*. Here *ryō* may be thought of as standing for the longer word.

As shown in figure 6 the character *hai* can be imagined as a depiction of a person clasping his hands together in prayer.

Many people go to temples to offer homage and to pray, while the sole purpose of others is to admire priceless works of art or the surroundings. In any case, anyone approaching a priest and wishing to be polite will say, *"Butsuzō o haikan sasete kudasai"*

("Please let me look at and worship the Buddhist images"). This rather than, *"Butsuzō o misete kudasai"* ("Please show me the Buddhist images"), which as you might guess, is rather brusque. As a matter of fact, a friend of mine was once refused a look at some beautiful works of art because he failed to use the more respectful way of speaking.

7. 徑 → 庭 → 庭 *tei*

It's not every temple that has both art and a garden, but after reverently contemplating *Butsuzō*, you may have a chance to enjoy a beautiful temple garden. Some temple gardens are famous for a particular feature. One, for example, maintains a rich variety of lush green moss, another a graceful bamboo forest; others offer the visitor absolutely nothing except sand and a few rocks, while many are at their best in a certain season, colorful autumn leaves, perhaps, or spring cherry blossoms reflected in a peaceful pond.

Figure 7 gives the character for *niwa*, "garden." Look closely at the upper portion and you will get the idea of an open area within a house. In the lower part a person is walking slowly. The open space came to mean a garden partially or wholly enclosed by a house.

8. 庭園 *teien*   9. 石庭 *sekitei*

In certain words, this kanji is pronounced *tei*, as in *teien*, where it is combined with the *en* of *kōen*, "park" (Fig. 8). This word, too, means "garden," but a *teien* is much larger than a *niwa* and one expects it to be more carefully planned and cared for.

Another form of *teien* is *sekitei*, literally a "rock garden" (Fig. 9). *Seki, ishi* means "rock," "stone" and *sekitei* is basically stones and rocks carefully located in a field of fine gravel. It can be likened to an abstract composition of islands afloat in a boundless sea, or nestled snugly in mountain streams and waterfalls. The simplicity and beauty of this kind of garden are said to express many of the ideals of Zen Buddhism, which repeatedly points a finger at the illusory nature of the phenomenal world and upholds detachment from phenomena as one step on the way to the higher levels of being—or non-being.

14

Castles and Museums

Other times you will have an opportunity to see gardens are when you visit the castles found in almost every part of Japan. *Shiro*, "castles" (Fig. 1), remnants from the days of the samurai, have existed for centuries, but regrettably those we see today are mostly reconstructions—often in exacting detail—of the great fortresses mostly built between the fifteenth and seventeenth centuries. Being fortresses, castles were surrounded by deep moats and raised on massive stone foundation walls. Being residences during times of peace, they dominated the towns that grew up around them to house the lord's lesser relatives and retainers and the merchants and artisans necessary to a thriving community.

1. 城 *jō*

Incorporated into a name, *shiro* becomes *jō*, as in *Edo-jō*, "Edo Castle," *Ōsaka-jō*, "Osaka Castle" and so on. The left side of this character is the radical for "earth." For the sake of memory, the right side can be thought of as men grouped for self-defense.

Four of these great fortresses are designated *Kokuhō*, "National Treasures." The oldest is Inuyama Castle near Nagoya. Another, Hikone Castle, stands on the shore of Lake Biwa. Himeji Castle (near Kobe), with its beautiful white walls, is traditionally said to resemble a graceful white heron. In contrast to Himeji Castle, Matsumoto Castle in Nagano Prefecture is widely known for its imposing black walls.

2. 江戸城 *Edojō*

A castle that no longer exists is Edo-jō (Fig. 2), but in the very heart of Tokyo where it once stood are the Imperial Palace and gardens. From this site the Tokugawa family, beginning with the powerful shogun Tokugawa Ieyasu, ruled from 1603 to 1867. Not all has been lost; most of the moat and some gate buildings remain, and some of the original structures are preserved at a temple long associated with the Tokugawas, Kitain in Kawagoe, Saitama Prefecture. The present inner buildings of the palace mostly date from this century.

Tokyo was called Edo in those days, and you will hear those 265 years referred to as both the Tokugawa period and the Edo period. But why Edo, you may ask. Judging from the meaning of the characters, two interpretations are possible. The first character could mean "a place where the sea enters (i.e., a bay)" or a "large river." Since the second character means "door," Edo could mean the "entrance" to a "bay" or to a "river." This seems to be a case where all of the above are true. Tokyo lies on Tokyo Bay and in the eastern part of the capital is the very substantial Ara-kawa, not to mention its navigable branch, the Sumida-gawa, and a host of interconnecting waterways.

3. 皇居 *kōkyo*

The place where the emperor lives is the Imperial Palace, surely, but, surprisingly, this is not a direct translation of the Japanese *kōkyo* (Fig. 3). The meaning of *kō* is "emperor," but *kyo* means only "residence." It occurs as a component of many common words where that meaning is intended. It is also the humble verb *i(ru)*, *o(ru)*, "to be," "to stay," "to reside."

4. 美術館 *bijutsukan*   5. → 美 → 美 *bi*

I'll close this chapter with a few more words that should come in handy when sightseeing.

Figure 4 shows the kanji for *bijutsukan*, "art museum." If you are a museum buff, here are a few names to get you started. Two of the top art museums are the Tokyo Metropolitan Art Museum and the National Museum of Western Art, both in Ueno. Among many fine private institutions are the Ohara Art Museum in Kurashiki, Okayama Prefecture, which boasts a great collection of Western painting, and the Kurita Art Museum (Tochigi Prefecture), known for its Imari and Nabeshima porcelains. The Gotō Art Museum in Tokyo is exceptional for its National Treasures in the form of the *Tale of Genji* scrolls. South of Tokyo is the MOA Museum of Art, which since 1982 has been exhibiting extensive Chinese and Japanese collections in a stunning mountainside building in the hot springs resort of Atami.

The *bi* seen in *bijutsukan* is also pronounced *utsuku(shii)*, "beautiful," "handsome," "noble" (Fig. 5). The top portion of this kanji depicts the head of a sheep and the lower part is *ō(kii)*, indicating "largeness." It may be amusing to think of a fat sheep as suggestive of beauty, but apparently the ancient Chinese seemed to consider a large sheep a particularly valuable animal.

The second character, *jutsu*, means "means," "technique" or "skill." The third character is one you have already seen in the word *ryokan* with its original meaning of a resting place for travelers. By and large, *kan* is used in the case of a large building of a type open to the public, whether publicly or privately owned.

6. 博物館 *hakubutsukan*　7. 民芸館 *mingeikan*

Shown in figure 6 is another *kan*, *hakubutsukan*, the term for "museum." Of course, there are many kinds of museums, but the National Museums in Tokyo, Kyoto and Nara are especially worth a visit, for their buildings have been constructed in traditional architectural styles and their exhibitions feature both National Treasures and noteworthy art from the world's greatest collections.

This *haku*, the first character, does not occur as an independent word, but it does have the meaning "wide ranging."

The second character, *butsu*, consists of the radical for *ushi*, "cow," on the left and on the right an element meaning "many colored." Imaginatively, you could consider the whole character to mean a multicolored cow. In fact, it is a good character to remember, for with either this pronunciation or as *mono*, "thing(s)," it crops up in many everyday words.

Yet another type of museum, increasingly popular in recent years, is *mingeikan*, the "folk craft museum" (Fig. 5). Their displays of folk crafts can be captivating, so there is a danger of being instantly changed into a collector. Among the more famous are folk craft museums in Takayama, Gifu Prefecture; Kurashiki, Okayama Prefecture; and Komaba in Tokyo.

Besides *kan*, one of the other characters in this compound should be familiar to you. The *min* was seen in *minshuku*, where, as you will recall, the meaning given was "general populace."

The new character here is, of course, *gei*, which means "art," "craft" or "technique." It derives from a sketch of a person planting a tree, in other words, practicing an agricultural technique. The other meanings evolved from this. (*See* chapter 29.)

8. 展覧会 *tenrankai*

At any of these museums, in department store exhibition halls, or on trains and many after places you will see announcements saying, *tenrankai*, "exhibition" (Fig 8). And with a little luck, if it has to do with Western art, you may find the artist's or the movement's name printed in English as well as Japanese.

The rather complicated characters making up *tenran* convey the basic meanings "to open" and "to show." It is possible to read the character for *ran* as *mi(ru)*, but the usual character for this is the one given in chapter 1 and seen here at the bottom of *ran*.

Kai is the *kai* of *kaisha*.

15
Geography

In the last few chapters I've given words connected with travel and sightseeing. Let's end this portion of the book with a short geography lesson.

As I have already mentioned, the Japanese archipelagos are made up of nearly four thousand small islands presided over by four large islands. The two main groups of islands are the Japanese Archipelago, forming a large arc off the coast of northeast Asia, and to the south the Ryukyu Archipelago, in which Okinawa is the biggest island.

1. 北海道 *Hokkaidō*   2. 本州 *Honshū*

Hokkaidō (Fig. 1), the northernmost major island, is second in size to *Honshū* (Fig. 2). It is twice as large as *Kyūshū* in the southwest. Unlike the other islands, it is blessed with wide open spaces, thus explaining why it has been called, "The Frontier of Japan." It has been a frontier in a second sense, too, having been opened to development only in the nineteenth century.

Here is a chance to know a word without learning any new characters. Starting with the first, we have the pronunciation *hoku* with the same meaning, "north," as *kita*. Next, as in *Nihon Kai*, the second character is *kai*, "sea." The last kanji you should remember as the *tō* of Shintō but here it is pronounced *dō* and has the assigned meaning "prefecture." *Hokkaidō* is, literally, the "prefecture in the northern sea."

The central island, *Honshū*, is the biggest (Fig. 2). Slightly smaller than the United Kingdom, it makes up three-fifths of the total land area of Japan.

In the *hon* of *Honshū*, we have for the first time the simple modification of another character, namely, *ki*, "tree." Adding a short horizontal stroke to the central vertical one in *ki* changes the meaning to "root," "base." Here it means "main."

Shū, also pronounced *su*, can mean quite different things, such as a large land mass, i.e., "continent," or political divisions of a country, i.e., "state," "province." This latter usage comes from an earlier meaning, "a place where people gather and live."

3. 四国 *Shikoku*　4. 九州 *Kyūshū*

The smallest of the principal islands, *Shikoku* (Fig. 3), is slightly less than half the size of *Kyūshū*. As you will see in the next chapter, the first character in this compound is *shi*, standing for the number "four." The second character, *koku*, "country," you have already met a couple of times. *Shikoku* was formerly divided into four provinces, each ruled by a *daimyō*, "feudal lord," and these became the four modern prefectures in 1871.

Kyūshū means "nine provinces" (Fig. 4). In this case, when provinces became prefectures, certain boundaries were redrawn and nine of the former ended up as seven of the latter. The island is no great distance from China and Korea, and *Kyūshū* was not only the first part of Japan to be exposed to foreign influences, but it conducted the only overseas trade during the long period of Tokugawa seclusion (1630s to 1850s).

5. 日本海 *Nihon Kai*　6. 太平洋 *Taiheiyō*

The sea filling up the space between Honshū and the Asian mainland is *Nihon Kai*, the "Sea of Japan" (Fig. 5). You should recognize all these characters.

Stretching thousands of kilometers to the east and south is *Taiheiyō*, the Pacific Ocean (Fig. 6).

The first character here is read *tai*, *futo(i)*, with the meanings "big" or "fat." Why this character was chosen for this word rather

than *ō(kii)*, "big," is a bit of a mystery until you know that the small dot added near the bottom of the *ō(kii)* character has the effect of changing the meaning to "bigger."

The second character is *hei*, *tai(ra)*, *hira* or *byō*, and means "peaceful" or "flat." The two characters combine to mean "tranquillity" or, as the very old sense of the Chinese has it, "(something) extremely peaceful and quiet."

Appropriately enough, the left side of the third character, *yō*, is the abbreviated character for "water." As seen in the upper part of the kanji for *utsuku(shii)*, the right side is the character for *hitsuji*, "sheep." The role of this radical here is to provide the pronunciation. There is only one, *yō*, and, rather unusually, it is the same for both the Chinese and the Japanese readings. In the former reading it means "sea," and in the latter it is much in evidence in words where the meaning "foreign," specifically "Western" or "European," is called for.

Whether by coincidence or otherwise, the meanings of *Taiheiyō* and *Pacific Ocean* do overlap considerably, the Japanese being "large, peaceful ocean," although at typhoon times it is anything but flat or peaceful. It is thought that *Taiheiyō* as a compound came into existence after Magellan crossed the South Pacific (1521) and word of his description of the ocean as peaceful and large reached Japan. In other words, this seems to be a rare case of an etymology closely paralleling that of the English term.

16
Numbers

The Japanese numbering system is as difficult as it is made out to be. For example, when flat, usually thin objects are counted, the suffix *mai* is added to each number to indicate this. We saw this in chapter 2 where train tickets were counted 1-*mai*, 2-*mai*, 3-*mai*, 4-*mai*. There are different suffixes for counting round objects, small animals, large animals, birds, ships, people, machines, tatami and so on. A couple of these counters, as they are called, come up in later chapters, but altogether there are too many to cover completely in this book. If you learn new ones as you encounter them, it should be sufficient.

1	2	3	4	5	6	7	8	9	10
一	二	三	四	五	六	七	八	九	十

ichi, ni, san, shi, go, roku, shichi, hachi, kyū, jū

11	12	13	14	15	16	17	18	19	20
十一	十二	十三	十四	十五	十六	十七	十八	十九	二十

jū-ichi, jū-ni, jū-san, jū-yon, jū-go, jū-roku, jū-shichi, jū-hachi, jū-kyū, nijū

21	22	23	24	25	26	27	28	29	30
二十一	二十二	二十三	二十四	二十五	二十六	二十七	二十八	二十九	三十

nijū-ichi, nijū-ni, nijū-san, nijū-yon, nijū-go, nijū-roku, nijū-shichi, nijū-hachi, nijū-kyū, sanjū

40	50	60	70	80	90	100	200	1,000	10,000
四十	五十	六十	七十	八十	九十	百	二百	千	万

yonjū, gojū, rokujū, nanajū, hachijū, kyūjū, hyaku, ni hyaku, sen, ichi man

1.

Reading the numbers themselves is not complicated and progresses to the higher ranges with mathematical regularity. Having learned the kanji from 1 to 10, you can recognize figures up to 99,999,999 by learning only three more symbols (Fig. 1). Beyond that, knowing two more kanji (*oku* for 100,000,000 and *chō* for 1,000,000,000,000) permits you to read into the trillions and beyond, high enough for anybody but astronomers, nuclear physicists and budgeteers.

To begin with, the cipher for zero used in English does quite nicely for Japanese, too. Number *ichi*, 1, is written by drawing a horizontal line, which some people say represents a pointing finger. I think of it as simply a horizontal 1.

Ni, 2, is written as two horizontal lines and *san*, 3, as three horizontal lines. After that a little rote memorization is called for.

From *jūichi*, 11, to *jūkyū*, 19, it is simple addition: the character for 10 plus the character for 1, 10 plus 2, 10 plus 3 and so on.

Nijū, 20, is literally "two tens," so the symbols are "2/10." Then again proceed by simple addition: for *nijūichi*, 21, you have 2/10/1, and so on up to 99.

百三十八	四百五十	六百三十五	千二百五十五	二千三百五	一万四百四十	一万一千七百
138	450	635	1255	2305	10440	11700

2.

三十六万八千五百四十九	五百三十二万七千八百六十八	九千三百四万五百五十五
368549	5327868	93040555

The characters for 100 and 1,000 came up earlier, although at that time I did not show how they are used in combination with other numbers. It's not so difficult; just continue to apply the same principle and put "x" hundred and/or "y" thousand in front of the numbers already learned. Note, however, that for "one" hundred and "one" thousand, the "one" is not written down. The respective kanji themselves mean "100" and "1000." (However, in legal documents, the "one" is expressed.)

That brings us up to 9,999, at which point you will probably feel exhausted. The Chinese of old may have felt the same way, or perhaps they were interested in saving space. Whatever the reason, they devised a different character for *ichi man*, 10,000. In this system, 20,000 is *ni man*, 2/10,000; 300,000 is *sanjū man*, 30/10,000; 4,000,000 is read as *yon hyaku man*, 4/100/10,000; and 50,000,000 is *go sen man*, 5/1,000/10,000. Study figure 2.

3. 円 *en*　　4. 千三百四十円 ¥1,340　　二千五百円 ¥2,500　　一万四百五十円 ¥10,450　　四万千六百七十二円 ¥41,672

Since Arabic numerals are widely used in Japan, why learn the Chinese system too, you may ask. A visit to a restaurant may be the quickest route to finding a reason. Eateries of many kinds— not just Chinese restaurants—use these kanji in their menus. Not being able to read the prices could lead to quite a shock when the time comes to pay the bill.

When it comes to expressing a certain amount of yen, there is a choice between the symbol, ¥, and the kanji *en* (Fig. 3). Use of the kanji, as shown in figure 4, is much favored among restaurateurs.

17

Noodles

In the next few chapters I will talk about food and restaurants in Japan. What and how people eat is undeniably an important aspect of culture, and many people regard eating as one of life's great joys. I hope the words and hints given here will enable you to walk into a restaurant and order with confidence, and that you will be able to thoroughly enjoy dining out in this country.

With a respectful bow toward China, where kanji originated, let's start with the Chinese restaurant. It is a little early to discuss the menus found at the fanciest places serving exotic dishes, where difficult kanji may be posers even for native speakers. Instead, let's take a look at the menu in a typical local Chinese restaurant.

1. 中国料理 *Chūgoku ryōri*   2. 中華料理 *Chūka ryōri*

Chūgoku ryōri, "Chinese food," also goes by the name of *Chūka ryōri* (Figs. 1–2). In Japanese, *Chūgoku* is a colloquial shortening of the country's full name, *Chūkajinmin Kyōwakoku*, "The Peoples' Republic of China." Although *Chūka* crops up in the names of some of the individual dishes, such as *Chūka soba*, "Chinese noodles," and *hiyashi Chūka*, "cold Chinese" noodles, the term *Chūgoku* is never used in this way.

3. 料理 *ryōri*

4. 𥹥 → 料 → 料 *ryō*

5. → 里 → 理 *ri*

The word *ryōri* spans meanings from prepared "dish" to

"cuisine" (Fig. 3). For example, put the name of a country in front of it and you have national styles, as in *Nihon ryōri*, "Japanese food," *Doitsu ryōri*, "German cooking," *Furansu ryōri*, "French cuisine" and so on.

The left side of the first character, *ryō*, is also pronounced *kome*, "(uncooked) rice" (Fig. 4). The right side is a symbol for *to*, an old unit of dry measure, so the kanji as a whole means "to measure out rice."

The second character in this combination is pronounced *ri* (Fig. 5). The left side of this *ri* is a picture of jewels strung on a string, and the right side depicts furrows neatly cut into a rice field. The idea is of making something in an orderly and straight manner by using a tool, perhaps one with an edge as fine as a jewel's. Similarly, in preparing food orderliness is a virtue.

One entry you will find on Chinese restaurant menus is *rāmen*, which is sometimes used in place of *Chūka soba*. These Chinese noodles were introduced in Tokyo at the end of the Meiji period (1868–1912).

6. 焼そば	7. 冷やし中華	8. 五目そば
yaki soba	*hiyashi Chūka*	*gomoku soba*

Based on this one type of Chinese noodle, there are a number of variations. One is *yaki soba*, "fried noodles" (Fig. 6), and another is the summer favorite *hiyashi Chūka* mentioned above (Fig. 7).

Whether regular, fried or cold, many noodle dishes are *gomoku soba* (Fig. 8). The meaning of *gomoku* is that there are "five items," but no need to take the number literally. There may be five or more ingredients selected from among such things as fish cake, spinach, chicken or pork, mushrooms, bamboo shoots, seaweed and so on. Each shop likes to do it its own way. A busy *Chūgoku ryōriya*, "Chinese restaurant," has most likely found a good combination.

If you have not been eating well because of the language barrier, I suggest you arm yourself with the vocabulary in figure 9 as a first step to variety.

ワンタンメン　　*wantanmen*, wonton and noodles

チャーシュー麺　*chāshūmen*, fried pork, noodles

タン麺　　　　　*tanmen*, vegetables, noodles

チャーハン　　　*chāhan*, fried rice

9.　酢豚　　　　*subuta*, sweet and sour pork

Noodles that are more traditionally Japanese are called *soba* or *udon*.

10. 日本そば *Nihon soba*

Soba, the "noodle," may have taken its name from *soba*, the "buckwheat" plant. Native to northeast Asia, buckwheat was brought from China or Korea, and has been cultivated in Japan since the third century B.C. It can be grown in any kind of soil and thrives best in a temperate climate. Famous for their *soba* grain made into good *soba* noodles are the northerly prefectures of Miyagi and Iwate, also, Nagano and Shimane prefectures, where the climate is influenced by the Sea of Japan. The names of such *soba* are known throughout Japan: Izumo, from Shimane; Shinshū, from Nagano; Wanko, from Iwate and so on.

Before assuming its present form, *soba* was made by adding hot water to plain buckwheat flour and was eaten just that way after a bit of stirring. Different methods of preparation began to appear in the seventeenth century. Since buckwheat flour by itself is not sticky enough to be rolled into noodles, it has to be mixed with other flour—barley or wheat—in the ratio of four to one. Then it can be kneaded and rolled into strips.

These long thin pale brown noodles are consumed in immense quantities every day of the week, but that does not keep them from being very popular at festivals and other celebrations. One reason for the popularity over the centuries is that they are considered a symbol of longevity, which is reflected in the old custom of welcoming the New Year with a midnight bowl of *toshikoshi soba*, roughly, "the year is spent noodles" . . . but, in the same breath, if another year is at hand let's not worry too much about the old one. (See *2nd Part*.)

Another occasion when noodles play a role is at moving time, when they are known as *hikkoshi soba*, "house-moving noodles," and are given to one's new neighbors. There is a play on words here in that *soba* written with a different kanji means "neighborhood." The act of giving acknowledges one's newness and is a humble request to be accepted.

11. 手打ちそば *teuchi soba*

The best noodles are made by hand and have a chewiness not duplicated in the machine-made variety. The noodle maker wields a single wooden roller, guided by technique acquired over many years, to roll the dough extremely thin. He then deftly slices it into very fine strips. To get the dough into the proper consistency for rolling and slicing, he kneads it by hand. Since the verb for "beat" is *u(tsu)*, this gives the *soba* the distinction of being *teuchi soba*, "hand-beaten noodles" (Fig. 11).

12. *uchi*

The left part of the kanji for *u(tsu)* signifies a hand and the right part a nail (Fig. 12). The meaning is to drive a nail with the hand, but unfortunately the name of the person who could do this has been lost in antiquity.

13. もりそば *mori soba*   14. ざるそば *zaru soba*

Two of the common offerings in noodle shops are *mori soba*, "noodles in good measure," and *zaru soba*, "noodles in a bamboo basket" (Figs. 13–14). Both these dishes are generally served on a shallow, square wooden plate or in a round shallow *zaru*, "bamboo basket," and there is little difference between them. If your noodles have a sprinkling of *nori* seaweed on top, you can be sure they are *zaru soba*.

15. そばつゆ *soba tsuyu*

When it comes to the important matter of taste, the secret of Japanese noodles is in the sauce into which they are dipped, mouthful by mouthful, while eating. Every noodle shop likes to think that its *tsuyu*, "broth," "soup," is the best (Fig. 15). Many shops claim to have guarded their recipes for generations, and indeed there are many possibilities. The taste derives from the stock, whose basic ingredients are soy sauce (several varieties), salt, sugar and sake (many, many varieties).

16. うどん *udon*

Udon, another traditional Japanese noodle, is made of wheat (Fig. 16). Wheat, along with barley, was introduced to Japan much later (third or fourth century A.D.) than buckwheat. According to the oldest recorded history of Japan, the *Kojiki*, the making of wheat flour dates from the Nara period (710–94). In those days preparation was a matter of shaping wheat flour into balls, filling these with vegetables or sweet bean paste, and then boiling them. It is unclear when *udon* noodles appeared, but we do know that it was somewhat before the beginning of the Edo period.

As you might imagine, hand-made *udon* is *teuchi* ("hand-beaten") *udon*. Nowadays there is only a handful of shops which serve these labor intensive noodles. Like *soba*, nearly all *udon* noodles come out of a machine.

17. なべ焼きうどん *nabeyaki udon*

While many dishes can be prepared using either *soba* or *udon*, udon is the sole choice for *nabeyaki udon*, "pot boiled noodles" (Fig. 17). To make this, the king of *udon* dishes, the noodles, other ingredients and broth are put into an earthenware pot. Other ingredients include *tempura* (deep fried vegetables, fish or meat), eggs, fish cake, meat, mushrooms and onions. Everything is boiled until the noodles absorb the flavor of the other ingredients. Whether cooked at the table or not, it is served piping hot and is a winter favorite, though eaten in summer too.

18. 燒 → 燒 → 焼 *yaki*

The *yaki* of *nabeyaki* is seen in the names of many foods and types of cooking. The verb is *ya(ku)*, "to burn," "to char," "to grill," "to bake," etc. (Fig. 18).

The left part of this kanji is the radical for *ka, hi,* "fire." Looking at the right side, imagine earth piled on a stand, symbolizing an oven. If you think of pottery stacked inside a kiln ready for the tremendous heat of firing, you'll easily be able to remember this character.

19. 薬味 *yakumi*

A little dish no bigger around than a teacup usually accompanies noodles. In it are one or more *yakumi*, "garnishes," "flavorings," "seasonings" (Fig. 19). For *soba* or *udon* these may be finely chopped onions, seaweed, red pepper or horseradish.

I will discuss these kanji later. For now simply keep in mind that *yaku, kusuri,* means "medicine," and *mi, aji,* means "taste." The linking of medicine and food may seem strange, but it probably goes back to a Buddhist idea that food was medicine and no more should be eaten than what is required to sustain life.

If you've wondered which type of restaurant is most common in Tokyo, investigation has revealed that noodle shops outnumber all other kinds. An interesting footnote here says that in the Kantō district *soba* shops lead *udon* shops in terms of total consumption. This is just the opposite of the situation in the Kansai district, where people tend to prefer *udon* to *soba*.

18
Restaurant and *Shokudō*

When poring over restaurant menus, chances are very good that you will come across many loanwords, so it will help if your *katakana* is in good working order. The word "restaurant" itself is just one example. In this case, the Japanese pronunciation, *resutoran*, is more similar to French than to English (Fig. 1).

1. 目黒レストラン
Meguro Resutoran

2. 目黒食堂
Meguro Shokudō

The reason for adopting this word was not lack of a Japanese equivalent. *Shokudō* is just one of several words for a public eating place (Fig. 2), and it is used just as widely as *resutoran*. To the inevitable question, "How do they differ?" there is no simple answer. If pressed, I would venture the opinion that *resutoran* summons up the image of a modern establishment, a chic interior and a menu centered on Western dishes. *Shokudō*, on the other hand, suggests a modest facility catering to the general public, with low prices and an informal atmosphere. The menu is mostly Japanese dishes with, perhaps, a few simple Western dishes as well. Maybe it can be said that the specialty of *shokudō* is non-specialization.

If you are looking for *shokudō*, the most likely locations are in or near stations, in department stores (usually top floor), college neighborhoods, and in or near office buildings.

A feature of every *shokudō* and lots of *resutoran* is *teishoku*, a "set meal" (Fig. 3). This is the equivalent of the French *table d'hote*, known in some quarters as the "daily special," although *teishoku* are almost always more appealing than the latter. These

3.

Meguro Shokudō

tonkatsu teishoku	¥600	(pork cutlet)
tempura teishoku	¥900	(tempura)
sashimi teishoku	¥850	(raw fish)

inexpensive meals may be either Western or Japanese. Broadly speaking, they are a combination of main and side dishes with rice or bread, maybe with soup, maybe with salad. They may or may not include a beverage. It's up to the cook.

4. 🥚 → 🍚 → 食 *shoku*

The first kanji in *teishoku* you know from having learned *teikiken*. The *shoku*, which you'll notice is the first character in *shokudō*, was seen in *ippaku nishoku*. As shown in figure 4, it depicts food in a lidded container. The *dō* in *shokudō* means "reception room," "hall" or "shop."

5. 天ぷら *tempura*   6. 🧍 → 天 → 天 *ten*

We've already seen words where characters are used for their pronunciation alone. *Tempura* is such a word. It can be written by using three kanji for their pronunciations, but the "spelling" shown in figure 5 is far more usual.

Tempura came to Japan with the first Westerners to live in this country, the Portuguese (mid 1500s), and has been eaten in its current form since around 1600. The original Portuguese word is

100

tempero, "seasoning," and it consists of vegetables or fish dipped in batter and deep fried. The best *tempura* is light and flaky, but this depends on the batter, which is made primarily from flour and water and is known as *koromo*, a high class word meaning "clothing."

The *kanji* still commonly seen in *tempura* is *ten*, "heaven," "sky" (Fig. 6). It is a picture of a man with a long line drawn above his head.

7. 丼 *donburi*　　8. 親子丼 *oyako donburi*

One small but nourishing standby you'll find in most *shokudō* is made by taking a bowl, filling it with rice, and giving it an easily prepared topping. The collective term for such dishes is *donburi*, "bowl" (Fig. 7). This character for *donburi* is not one of the *Jōyō Kanji*, but it couldn't be easier to remember; it resembles a last lone grain of rice in a bowl. (*Jōyō Kanji* are the 1,945 characters officially recognized by the Ministry of Education for use in newspapers, periodicals and school curricula.)

One *donburi* answers the old question, which came first, the chicken or the egg? They both come at the same time if you order *oyako donburi* (Fig 8). The word-for-word name for this chicken-and-egg-on-rice dish is "parent-child bowl."

9. 親 → 親 → 親 *oya*　　10. 子 → 子 → 子 *ko*

Oyako is a compound of *oya*, "parent," and *ko*, "child," so you can see its appropriateness (Fig. 9). The left side of *oya* comes from a sketch of a person standing and a tree, and the right side is, of course, *mi(ru)*, "to see." The overall meaning is to watch over carefully, just as parents do with their children. This kanji also means *shita(shii)*, "intimate," "familiar."

The character for *ko(-go)*, *shi*, "child," is quite simple and straightforward; it evolved directly from a sketch of a child (Fig. 10).

11. 玉子丼 *tamago donburi*   12. 8 → 王 → 玉 *tama*   卵

Eggs without the chicken is your second option. This is called *tamago*, "egg," *donburi*, but most people shorten it to *tamago-don* (Fig. 11).

Tamago combines *tama(-dama)*, "jewel," "ball," with *-go*, "child" (Fig. 12). *Tama* represents three jewels strung together, as noted previously, to which is added a dot. (Without the dot, the kanji is the radical *ō*, "king.") Figure 12 also shows how *tamago* can be written with a single character, but this is much less likely to be found in a menu.

Other *donburi* get their names clipped a bit too, for example, *tendon* for *tempura donburi*. Study figure 13 and increase the variety in your diet a little bit more.

天丼   *tendon* (tempura)

カツ丼   *katsudon* (pork cutlet)

13. 中華丼   *Chūkadon* (Chinese style)

Although narrower in smaller cities, the gamut of restaurants in Tokyo catering to Western tastes goes from *haute cuisine* to the affordable but thoroughly domesticated type. In the lower ranges, you should not be surprised to find seaweed in your spaghetti, a bean jam filling in your Danish or green tea flavoring your ice cream. (The last, by the way, is a wonderful summer treat.)

Meat has been available in Japan for centuries, but because of religious beliefs eating it was much frowned upon. Consumption by the general populace dates from the late nineteenth century. At present, fish still has a statistical lead over meat, but the gap is narrowing and there are more and more younger Japanese who prefer meat to fish. This will become quite obvious when you learn to recognize the characters for beef, pork and meat and realize just how ubiquitous they really are.

14. $gy\bar{u}$ 15. *buta*

16. *niku*

The origins of $gy\bar{u}$, *ushi*, "cow," "beef"; *buta*, "pig," "pork"; and *niku*, "meat," are shown in figures 14–16. The kanji for $gy\bar{u}$ and *niku* came from depictions of a cow's head and horns and a slice of meat, respectively. The kanji for *buta* has the abbreviated form of *niku* on the left and the radical for *inoko*, "hog," on the right. The latter started out as a picture of a pig.

Incidentally, if the word *niku* is used without specification, the meat is more likely to be pork. And along with *buta* something or other, you may find the loanword *hamu*, "ham," on the same menu. Also *raisu* for "rice." Of course, the proper word for "rice" is *gohan*, so long as it is served in a bowl. When rice is served on a plate—this may be done in Chinese as well as Western style eateries—it automatically becomes *raisu*.

In figure 17 are a few everyday dishes typical of *resutoran* and *shokudō* fare.

サービス・ランチ	*sābisu ranchī*, lunch special
牛肉のしょうが焼き	*gyūniku no shōgayaki*, beef and ginger, fried
豚肉のしょうが焼き	*butaniku no shōgayaki*, pork and ginger, fried
ライス	*raisu*, rice
ハンバーガーステーキ	*hanbāgā sutēki*, hamburger steak
ミックス・ピザ	*mikkusu piza*, mixed pizza
ドライカレー	*dorai karē*, dry curried rice
17. グラタン	*guratin*, gratin (casserole)

103

19
Grilled Chicken and Raw Fish

Specialty restaurants are very much a part of the Japanese scene. Two of these are the *yakitoriya* (Fig. 1) and the *sushiya*.

One segment of the population *yakitoriya* are hugely popular with is composed of businessmen and office-workers. After a hard day's work, stopping off on the way home for snacks and a drink is just short of a ritual. The smallest of these shops seat a dozen customers or less, so they fill up rapidly, but reasonable prices and an expert chef grilling skewered meat over glowing charcoal make for a relaxing atmosphere to be shared with friends and colleagues.

The secret of good *yakitori*, according to many, lies in *tare*, the basting sauce composed essentially of soy sauce, sugar and sake.

1. 焼き鳥 やきとり *yakitori*   2. → 𦥑 → 鳥 *tori*

The character for *tori* is given in figure 2. Remember *shima*, "island"? As noted in chapter 11 these two kanji are the same except for the bottom part. In *tori*, also pronounced *chō*, you might think of the four dots as being a bird's footprints. *Tori* is the usual word for "bird," and the character forms part of the names of many birds. When the context is food, it always means "chicken."

Despite the name, not all *yakitori*, whether flesh or innards, comes from two-footed birds. Depending on the shop, certain items on the menu may very well be from four-footed animals. In fact, I have been to many *yakitoriya* where everything was from the pig.

Yaki was explained in chapter 17 in connection with *nabeyaki*. Study the items in figures 3–8 and the comments that follow for some additional examples of usage.

3. すき焼き　*sukiyaki*   6. 鉄板焼き　*teppanyaki*

4. かば焼き　*kabayaki*   7. 焼きそば　*yaki soba*

5. お好み焼き　*okonomiyaki*   8. 目玉焼き　*medamayaki*

Sukiyaki is well-known outside Japan, so there is no need to explain it beyond mentioning that, yes, it is eaten even in Japan, and it is a wonderful way to enjoy beef fried lightly in a skillet with vegetables (Fig. 3).

Kabayaki is eel basted with a special sauce while being grilled (Fig. 4). It is difficult to prepare and it is generally served on top of rice. Then, it is often called *unadon*, (*unagi* ["eel"] *donburi*).

Okonomiyaki means "grilled as you like it" (Fig. 5). This is a pancake stuffed with a mixture of cabbage and—diner's choice—beef, pork, shrimp and so on. When the grilling is finished, each pancake is topped off with the shop's own special sauce (sweet or tart) and condiments like chopped seaweed or ground red pepper.

In *teppanyaki*, we see the kanji *tetsu*, "iron" and *han(-pan)*, "sheet" or "board" (Fig. 6). *Okonomiyaki* is cooked on these large thick grills. As the name of a style of cooking *teppanyaki* involves using the same type of grill to fry a variety of meats, seafoods and vegetables cut into chunks.

Yaki soba, noted previously as an example of Chinese food, is noodles pan-fried with vegetables and bits of meat (Fig. 7). Or it may be cooked on a *teppanyaki* grill. Both *okonomiyakiya* and *teppanyakiya* commonly serve *yaki soba*.

Medamayaki, written with familiar kanji, is the moniker for eggs sunny side up. *Medama* does mean "eyeball," so it is an imaginative name. Come to think of it, the English term is fanciful too, isn't it? Anyway, if you want rice with your fried eggs, you'll have to order it separately.

Like sukiyaki, *sushi* is well liked at home and abroad. The forerunner of *sushi*, a method of preserving fish by salting and fermentation, was adopted in Japan at least as early as the tenth century. At first, rice was thrown away after playing its role in the fermentation process; only the fish was eaten. Eating both rice and fish became the custom from around the sixteenth century.

Su, "vinegar," is important in making *sushi*, a word that originally denoted both vinegared fish or shellfish and fish or shellfish with vinegared rice (the present meaning).

9. すし *sushi*   10. 寿司 *sushi*   11. 鮨 *sushi*

Figures 9–11 show the three ways of writing *sushi* as seen in signs and on *noren* shop curtains. The two kanji in figure 10 are like *hiragana* in that they provide pronunciation only. However, some sushi lovers believe that the inclusion of the first character, *su*, *kotobuki*, "long life" or "congratulations," is a hint that the more sushi you eat the longer you will live. And this may be true, since *sushi* is a very healthfully nutritious food. The meaning of the second character, *shi*, is "official," "government official."

With the kanji in figure 11, we get down to business. On the left it has the radical *uo*, *sakana*, "fish" and on the right *shi*, *uma(i)*, "delicious." Yet this character is not among the Jōyō Kanji and, in fact, only two kanji incorporating the fish radical are on the officially recognized list. These two are *azaya(ka)*, "fresh," "beautiful," and *kujira*, "whale." Paradoxically, neither is the name of a fish.

Although there are several dozen characters with the fish radical, only a few combine with other kanji to form a handful of words, and this, apparently, is the reason for their being off the list. But being in a state of limbo, so to speak, does not keep them from appearing prominently in such places as sushi shops.

12. 鰯 *iwashi*

To take but one example look at the word *iwashi*, "sardine" (Fig. 12). This made-in-Japan character brings together *sakana*, "fish" and *yowa(i)*, which can mean either "tender" or "weak." The latter certainly applies here. Sardines die as soon as they are out of water.

Variety and innovation are hallmarks of *sushi*. Among the many varieties, the two best known styles are those of Tokyo, *nigiri-zushi*, "(hand) shaped sushi," and Osaka, *Ōsaka-zushi*. The latter consists of sweetened vegetables or fish in an omeletlike or seaweed wrapper.

Nigiri-zushi is also called *Edomae-zushi*, "in front of Edo sushi." What's in front of Edo (Tokyo) is Tokyo (formerly Edo) Bay, once a source of fish for the capital. In these days of huge demand, fish are imported from points near and far with Japan still leading the world in food fishing.

In figure 13 I have listed a few more types of *sushi*. I hope this will be useful to you.

いなりずし *inari-zushi*, rice in a thin wrapper of fried bean curd

のりまき *nori-maki*, rice rolled around vegetables in a seaweed wrapper

てっかまき *tekka-maki*, rice rolled around tuna in a seaweed wrapper

おしんこまき *o-shinko-maki*, rice rolled around pickled vegetables in a seaweed wrapper

しそまき *shiso-maki*, rice rolled around *shiso* leaf in a seaweed wrapper

ちらし *chirashi-zushi*, fish and vegetables arranged on a bowl of rice

にぎりずし *nigiri-zushi*, raw fish on finger-shaped vinegared rice

13. 玉子まき *tamago-maki*, rice rolled around vegetables or fish in an omelet wrapper

20

A Glassful, a Bottle

It wouldn't do to overlook that inseparable companion of *yakitori* and *sushi*, namely, *sake*. I'll discuss Japan's traditional drink more fully in the *2nd Part*; here I'd like to give you the

overall picture and tell you how to count your glassfuls and your
bottles, empty or full.

1. 氵☖ → 氵酉 → 酒 *sake*   2. 日本酒 *Nihonshu*

The kanji for *sake*, also pronounced *shu*, is shown in figure 1. It
combines the idea of flowing water, which is of prime importance
in sake making, on the left side with an earthen pot filled with
sake on the right side. An alternative name for this traditional
beverage is *Nihonshu*, a term frequently called upon to avoid am-
biguity (Fig. 2), since *sake* is a generic term. (You will also hear
sake pronounced *saka* in such words as *sakaba*, "bar," and
sakaya, "liquor store.")

3. ウイスキー   4. ぶどう酒／ワイン   5. 焼酎
   uisukī   *budōshu/wain*   *shōchū*

Sake, or *o-sake*, with the meaning of "alcoholic beverages" is
seen on the great majority of menus in Japan. In this section of the
menu, you'll find, besides *Nihonshu*, such standbys as domestic
and imported *uisukī*, "whiskey"; *wain/budōshu*, "wine"/"grape
wine"; *bīru*, "beer"; and a liquor called *shōchū* (Figs. 3–5). This
last has no equivalent in English. Currently enjoying a tremendous boom in Japan, it is like gin and vodka in being colorless
and, in its traditional form, potent, although it has been toned
down for the mass urban market. One of the two basic types is virtually tasteless and is generally mixed with a fruit-based flavoring.
Shōchu is distilled from one of several materials, mainly grains,
rice, corn, sugar cane or potatoes.

6. 生ビール *nama bīru*   7. 屮 → 㞢 → 生 *nama*

These days, so-called draft beer comes in bottles as well as out
of a tap. Either way, the term to know is *nama bīru*, "fresh (draft)
beer" (Fig. 6). The character *nama* represents a plant shoot break-

ing above the ground (Fig. 7). This kanji, with a total of ¦
has the largest number of readings of any kanji in comm¦
Some of these are *sei*, *shō*, *i(kiru)*, "life," "live"; *u(mare)*, "birth";
ki-, "pure"; and *na(ru)*, "grow." For now, remember the pronunciation *nama* and its meanings of "uncooked" and "raw," which
occur in expressions like *nama-zakana*, "raw fish," and *nama
yasai*, "raw vegetables."

I mentioned counters, the suffixes that give an indication of
what is being counted, in chapter 16. When ordering a drink in
Japan, you will want to make a distinction between two of these
counters, one indicating glass(es) filled with any liquid and the
other referring, in the present context, to bottles.

To order a glass of anything, the suffix is *-hai* (*-bai*, *-pai*). Starting with "one glassful," this series goes: 1, *ippai*; 2, *nihai*; 3, *sanbai*; 4, *yonhai*; 5, *gohai*; 6, *roppai*; 7, *nanahai*; 8, *happai*; 9, *kyū-
hai*; and 10, *juppai*. Among other things counted this way are cup-
fuls and bowlfuls.

The following sentence should help you remember this usage.

8. 水割りを三ばい下さい

Mizu-wari o sanbai kudasai. "Three (water) highballs, please."

By the way, the second syllable in *ippai* is written like the second syllable in a word you won't want to be without when you
go drinking: *Kampai*, "Cheers!"

When you are ordering beer, whiskey, mineral water, sake or
whatever it is by the bottle, the counter is *-hon* (*-bon*, *-pon*), as
follows: 1, *ippon*; 2, *nihon*; 3, *sanbon*; 4, *yonhon*; 5, *gohon*; 6,
roppon; 7, *nanahon*; 8, *happon*; 9, *kyūhon*; and 10, *juppon*.
Besides bottles, the counter *-hon* is used for almost anything long,
such as cigarettes, pencils, trees, neckties, etc.

9. 日本酒を三本下さい

Nihonshu o sanbon kudasai. "Three bottles/ceramic warmers of sake,
please."

109

21
Open for Business

In this chapter I'd like to say a few words about coffee shops, box lunches and certain signs displayed by shopkeepers.

The coffee shop, sitting like an oasis in the midst of urban bustle, is a place for doing many things besides the obvious one of having a cup of coffee or tea. It is a place to collect oneself in those last few minutes before an interview, to mull over a meeting just finished, to have small informal discussions, to meet friends, to sit and read undisturbed, to listen to music, to relax or just to while away the time. All sorts of people find coffee shops a great convenience, so they exist in great numbers. In Tokyo alone there are so many that, at the rate of one a day, it might very well take the rest of your life to visit each and every one of them.

1. 喫茶店 *kissaten*

The full pronunciation of the first character in *kissaten* is *kitsu*, which encompasses the meanings "drinking" and "smoking" (Fig. 1). This character is also frequently seen on the sign *kitsuen shitsu*, "smoking room," in movie theaters and playhouses. Remembering that the upper half can be divided into three parts and that the left element is *kuchi*, "mouth," should be helpful in quickly recognizing this rather difficult kanji.

2. 茶茶 → 茶茶 → 茶 *sa*　　3. 仚仚 → 占 → 店 *ten*

The second character, here pronounced *sa*, is more familiar as *cha*, "tea" (Fig. 2). This kanji combines the radical *kusa*, "grass," at the top with a bottom part that supplies the pronunciation. This is the *cha* seen in *o-cha*, "green tea" (made from unfermented leaves) and *kocha*, "black tea" (made from fermented leaves) and quite a number of words related to tea drinking and *cha no yu*, the "tea ceremony."

The third character, *ten, mise*, means "shop," "store" (Fig. 3). With a little imagination you can see at top and left the outline of a house, open on the right side like a shop. Within is the character for *uranai*, "fortune-telling," representing a crack in a turtle's shell plus a mouth. In other words, a shop can be thought of as a house where goods are lined up and sold, much as the fortune-teller lines up his charts and sells his words of prediction.

The business of *kissaten* is primarily to quench the customer's thirst. Besides coffee, black tea, fruit juices and milk drinks, coffee shops may serve ice cream and cake, sandwiches and other light snacks. The menu will tell you. Below is a sample of their offerings.

コーヒー *kōhī,* coffee   クリームソーダ *kurīmu sōda,* cream soda

ココア   *kokoa,* cocoa   コカコーラ *koka-kōra,* Coca-cola

4. オレンジジュース *orenji jūsu,* orange juice

Speaking of light snacks, this is a good place to mention a certain type of fast-food place whose popularity has been mushrooming in recent years. If you've traveled by train, you've probably seen the box lunches sold on board or on the station platform. The same type of meal is now available from *bentōya*, the "box-lunch shops" that have sprung up in many locations, including business districts. These lunches are typically built around rice with the other foods being fried or grilled fish, meat or chicken, eggs, vegetables, pickles and a variety of other things. Many shops have *o-nigiri* and *sushi*.

5. 弁当 *bentō*

Both characters in *bentō* are there merely for the sake of phonetics (Fig. 5). For your information, *ben* has such meanings as *ben(zuru)*, "to speak," "to distinguish," and *tō* means, for example, "appropriateness." As you can see, no relation to the edible *bentō*.

Have you ever headed for a favorite restaurant or coffee shop and been greeted by an incomprehensible sign hanging on the doorknob? Was it still morning and you had no way of knowing whether the place was getting ready to open or would be closed for the whole day? If you learn to read the following signs, you'll have a better idea of what's going on.

6. 営業中 *eigyōchū*

7. 營 → 營 → 営 *ei*

8. 業 → 業 → 業 *gyō*

The sign in figure 6 lets you know that the store is open and ready for business. It says exactly that: *eigyōchū*, "(open for) business."

I gave the meaning of the first character in connection with *Eidan Sen*, i.e., *ei*, *itona(mu)*, "to operate," "to run." It is said that this character evolved with the two characters at the top (*hi*, "fire") representing two fireflies flying around two houses surrounded by a wall (Fig. 7). According to legend, the Japanese used to study by the light of fireflies, thus this character's basic meaning of "to act," "to perform." I sympathize with future instructors who have to make this explanation. With pollution killing off fireflies so fast, few of their students will even know what a firefly is.

The second character in this compound is pronounced *gyō* or *waza*, and means "work," "occupation," "business," or "industry" (Fig. 8). Originally this character depicted the stands from which bells, drums and the like were hung. At one time the meaning was "difficult work," and since technique or skill is called for when things are difficult, it came to mean "performance," "art," "profession." This kanji occurs in many words having to do with business, commerce and industry, including *eigyō*, one term meaning "business" or "operation."

The last character, *chū*, you have seen before. As is the case here, it is added to many words to convey the idea of being in the "middle" of or "in the process of" doing something.

9. 準備中 *junbichū*   10. 𤝐→偹→備 *bi*

The store displaying the sign in figure 9 is not open yet but will be before long. This sign says, *junbichū*, "preparing (to open)."

The meaning of the character *jun*, "standard" or "aim," does not really contribute to the meaning of the whole word, so you'll just have to remember it by rote.

The second kanji, *bi, sona(eru)*, by itself has the meaning "to prepare," "to provide," "to furnish" (Fig. 10). It evolved from the depiction of a man next to a case for arrows, readying himself, no doubt, for their future use.

11. 本日は終了しました *Honjitsu wa shūryō shimashita.*

Simply put, the notice shown in Fig. 11 says you're out of luck today; it is after closing time.

The first two kanji here are read *honjitsu*, "today," literally, "this day," and are the two characters seen in *Nihon*, "Japan," in reverse order.

The second compound, pronounced *shūryō*, meaning "end," "completion," "conclusion," is converted into a verb by adding *suru*, which in this announcement has become the past tense *shimashita*. The first character *owa(ri)*, *shū*, has these same meanings. On the left is a picture of thread, and on the right we have the character for winter. The thread is completely wrapped around a spool, and the kanji originally represented tying off a coil of thread. Later it came to mean "finish."

This compound is another case of having the meaning doubled. *Ryō*, too, means "completely done," "concluded."

113

12. 本日休業 *honjitsu kyūgyō* 13. 定休日 *teikyūbi*

In figures 12 and 13 we see sign words made of kanji already introduced. Can you figure them out?

Literally, *honjitsu* means "today," as noted above, and *kyūgyō* means "rest (from) business" (Fig. 12). The term is used in situations ranging from the periodic rest day any store or business has, hence "closed for the day," to "suspension of business" for whatever reason.

Teikyūbi, "regular day (of) rest," on the other hand, is unambiguous, incorporating as it does the *tei* of *teikiken* and *teishoku* plus *yasumi*, "rest," and *bi*, *hi*, "day" (Fig. 13).

Let me end these few chapters on dining out in Japan with a sign you may find in place of something you wanted to purchase. If the lunch hour gets busy enough, you may even see it in your favorite restaurant.

14. 売り切れ *urikire*

Urikire means "sold out" (Fig. 14). For now it is enough to know that this term is a compound of two verbs, *u(ru)*, "to sell," and *ki(reru)*, "to expire," "to be out of." You probably already know that vending machines are programmed to flash this information when their stock of cigarettes, soft drinks, beer or what have you is gone.

22
Post Office

Knowing the appropriate words will take all the confusion out of mailing letters and parcels, but before going inside the post office, let's take a look at *yūbin posuto*, the public "mailbox" (Fig. 1).

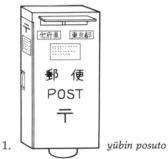

1.   *yūbin posuto*

Standing on a single pillar and painted orange, the big-city mailbox has two slots and a printed schedule of the pick-up times. If you remember the characters for *heijitsu*, "weekday," and *kyū-jitsu*, "holiday," you should be able to decipher the schedule.

2. 他府県 *ta-fu-ken*   3. 東京都 *Tōkyō-to*

Figures 2 and 3 give the words found under the left and right slots of a typical Tokyo mailbox. The kanji on the right, *Tōkyō-to*, "Tokyo Metropolitan Prefecture," have all been introduced. Into this slot goes mail bound for any address in the twenty-three wards, twenty-six cities, seven towns, eight villages, one county and seven small Pacific islands that make up the prefecture.

Since we find under the left slot the compound *ta-fu-ken*, "other prefectures-prefectures," a word of explanation is in order. Japan has all together forty-seven prefectures. Forty-three of these are *ken* prefectures. Two others are *Tōkyō-to* and *Hokkai-dō*. The remaining two are *Ōsaka-fu* and *Kyōto-fu*, both locations of former capitals. (Tokyo was a *fu* from 1888 until 1943, when it was renamed *to*.) Although the official designations preserve historical shadings, there is now no difference between prefectures in their relationship to the national government.

4. 狼 → 他 → 他 *ta*   5. 府 *fu*   6. 県 *ken*

The *ta*, "other," of *ta-fu-ken* consists of the radical for *hito*, "man," on the left side and, according to the source, a poisonous snake or a scorpion on the right (Fig. 4). As legend has it, the meaning came from a certain man's hope, upon running into a poisonous snake, that the snake would go in some other direction.

Fu, "urban prefecture," developed as a character with the meaning "storehouse" (Fig. 5). Since rice was kept in government storehouses in olden days, this kanji took on the meaning of an administrative (government) office. Today, the majority of words it is part of have to do with Kyoto and Osaka prefectures.

Ken, "prefecture," is a kanji having a single pronunciation (Fig. 6). It was used long ago in China to designate an administrative district and now occurs in a number of words having to do with prefectures, their people and their affairs.

7. 郵便 *yūbin*

On the front of the mailbox in raised letters you will find, besides "Post," the characters for *yūbin*, "mail," "postal service" (Fig. 7).

The first character in *yūbin* represents a banner once used to signal information between villages. Associated with this was the idea of "sending" or "delivering." The foundations of the modern postal system, a great improvement on previous methods, were established in 1873.

The second character in *yūbin* is also pronounced *ben* and has the basic meaning "convenient." The left side is the radical for "man." The right side derives from elements symbolizing stretching and motion, on the basis of which the character can mean "to reform," "to remedy."

A handy way to recall *yūbin* is to think of written messages conveniently delivered.

The only reason a lot of foreigners in Japan ever go to a post office is to buy ordinary stamps. Actually, there is an added inducement in the great many beautiful *kinen kitte*, "commemorative stamps," issued by the Ministry of Posts and Telecommunications (*Yūseishō*). Festivals, National Treasures, sports, the arts, wildlife and fish are among the motifs, and the stamps are so extremely popular that they are frequently sold out on the day of issue. Naturally, it is a case of the early bird gets the worm, and when you get to the head of the line you can put the sentence in figure 8 to use. Alternatively, you can order commemorative issues in advance at the Tokyo Central Post Office, or other main post offices, and have them mailed to you.

8. 記念切手を十まいください   9. 切手
   Kinen kitte o jū-mai kudasai.   *kitte*

For ordinary stamps, look for the window with the characters *kitte*, "stamp," above it (Fig. 9). Air letters and *hagaki*, "postcards," are obtainable at the same window. To get the former, brush up your *katakana* pronunciation and say, *ēroguramu* or *eyaretā*. If you want to impress the clerk you can do so by making use of the direct translation of "air letter" into Japanese, *kōkūshokan*.

10. ki(ru)

The first character in *kitte* was seen in the previous chapter in *urikire*, meaning, "sold out." Here it stands for the verb *ki(ru)*, "to cut." Some say the left side is a stick of freshly cut wood. To provide the means for cutting, the right side of this character is the kanji for *katana*, "sword" (Fig. 10).

The second character in this combination is, of course, *te*, "hand."

To mail a package, go to the counter under the sign shown in figure 11.

11. 小包 *kozutsumi*   12. → 包 *tsutsumi*

Since the first kanji, *ko*, "small," is not new to you, let's go on to the second.

Tsutsu(mu), *tsutsu(mi)(-zutsu[mi])*, meaning "to wrap" and "bundle," "parcel," respectively, evolved from the shape of a person wrapping a child in his stomach, perhaps to protect it (Fig. 12).

Together, these kanji form *kozutsu(mi)*, "small package," the size the mailman looks most favorably on.

In figure 13 are a couple of sentences that will come in handy when mailing packages overseas.

(パリ)までこの小包を(こうくうびん)
でおねがいします

(Pari) made kono kozutsumi o (kōkūbin) de onegai shimasu.
"I'd like to send this package to (Paris) by (airmail), please."

（サンフランシスコ）までこの小包を
13. (ふなびん)でおねがいします

(San Furanshisuco) made kono kozutsumi o (funabin) de onegai shimasu.
"I'd like to send this package to (San Francisco) by (seamail), please."

The peak in overseas mailing is seen, of course, in the weeks before Christmas, and each year the post office puts up notices giving the deadlines by continent and country. Those living in the Tokyo area may want to drop their holiday mail off at the Tokyo International Post Office. Surprisingly, a large number of people have never heard of it, but going there may save time, since all overseas mail from the surrounding area is funneled through this facility. It is located a short walk north from the Marunouchi North Exit of Tokyo Station.

14. 国際郵便局 kokusai yūbin kyoku

Kokusai Yūbin Kyoku in figure 14 means "International Post Office." The *koku* of *kokusai*, as you saw in *Kokutetsu*, means "country."

The second character, with the pronunciation *sai* or *kiwa*, has the meanings "time," "occasion" or "side," "edge." It has several elements, but they sum up to suggest neighboring mountains and the meaning "to meet" or, going a little further, "to have social relationships with." The quickest way to recognize this kanji is by the right side, which is pronounced *sai* or *matsuri*, "festival," a time when people rub shoulders with each other and enjoy it immensely.

The *kyoku* added to the end of this phrase means "bureau," "office." It is added to many words and is very often evidence of a bureaucracy at work.

15. 中央郵便局 chūō yūbin kyoku

Walking from Tokyo International Post Office back past Tokyo Station to Marunouchi South Exit puts you across the street from *Tōkyō Chūō Yūbin Kyoku*, Japan's largest. As you can see in figure 15, *chūō*, "central," is the same as in *Chūō Sen*.

Post offices provide some non-postal services. One is postal savings accounts, both ordinary and long-term. They are also a place where utility bills can be paid, a service that certain banks offer, too. I'll discuss this in a later chapter.

One of the special postal services I would like to mention here is *sokutatsu*, "special delivery." This costs ¥200 more than the normal cost for a letter (currently ¥60) or a postcard (currently ¥40). To ask for this use the sentence in figure 16. Note that the *soku* is the same kanji as in *kaisoku*, "fast (train)."

16. 速達でお願いします *sokutatsu de onegai shimasu.*

There are three or four ways to remit money by mail. The most direct and convenient, especially for the receiver, is called *genkin kakitome*, "registered cash." You can mail up to ¥100,000 in one specially designed *fūtō*, "envelope," for a fee of ¥410–590, depending on the amount of money enclosed. First you must obtain the envelope, which costs ¥20. The sentence in figure 17 should accomplish this. Then you write the addressee's name and address, as well as your own, in the appropriate places on the envelope and insert the money. When you take the envelope back to the counter, the clerk will tell you how much you have to pay and give you a receipt for the envelope.

17. 現金書留の封筒をください *Genkin kakitome no fūtō o kudasai.*

The procedure for other registered mail is similar to this, except that no special envelope is necessary. The post office will accept any ordinary envelope or suitably wrapped parcel. Simply say, *Kakitome de onegaishimasu.*

23
Basics of Banking

Japan has a complex web of domestic and foreign banking and financial institutions. The Bank of Japan (the central bank) and certain key banks are under direct government control, but all banks, public and private, are strictly regulated in such matters as interest rates and hours of operation. Most individuals choose a bank that is conveniently located, serves their particular needs, and provides satisfactory service.

Standard banking hours are from 9 A.M. to 3 P.M. weekdays, although one type of savings bank is permitted to stay open until 6 P.M. On Sundays and legal holidays the banks are closed. In keeping with the movement towards a five-day workweek, banks are presently closed on the second and third Saturdays of each month. On the Saturdays they are open, the hours are 9 A.M. to 12 noon, again with the savings bank having somewhat longer hours.

Standard hours are extended a bit by the banks' automatic teller machines (ATMs). These are accessible to the public fifteen minutes or a half hour before and up to three or four hours after the standard banking hours, even though the bank itself is closed. Cash dispensers (CDs, withdrawals only) are located at banks, shopping areas, department stores, stations and so on and have similar hours. Withdrawals can be made through either the ATM or the CD even on those Saturdays when the banks are closed.

1. 銀行 *ginkō*

The word for "bank" is *ginkō* (Fig. 1). It consists of two characters already seen, the *gin* of *Ginza* and the *kō* of *kyūkō*, "express (train)."

Since *gin* means "silver," it might, perhaps, seem more logical for the character *kin*, "gold," to be chosen in writing the word for "bank," but as noted in discussing the *ryō* in *ryōgae*, during the Edo period silver enjoyed an edge as a medium of exchange.

Just as *Ginza* can be remembered as the "seat of silver," *ginkō* is the place where "silver goes."

Banks have two types of windows, so to speak. You'll easily recognize the tellers' windows as being like the ones in your own country. Besides these, there will be a lower counter, or desks, with chairs on the customer's side. You go to one of these to open an account or to consult about banking services. The signs will tell you which are for what purpose. The one you'll want first has the word shown in figure 2.

121

2. ご相談 *go-sōdan*

The *go* in *go-sōdan* is an honorific prefix. Its presence at the beginning of a word indicates that the speaker or writer wishes to show respect towards the listener or reader. In this case, the bank is showing deference towards all its honorable customers.

3. 𝄇 → 相 → 相 *sō*   4. 𝄇 → 言 → 談 *dan*

The first character of *sōdan*, pronounced *sō* or *ai*, is made up of the characters for *ki*, "tree," and *me*, "eye" (Fig. 3). When you climb to the top of a tree you can see well. It therefore became associated with the idea of what's right before one's eyes, that is, appearance or shape. From the idea that you can see a person best face to face came the concept of "mutual," "reciprocal," and there are a number of compounds besides this one in which it conveys this meaning.

The *dan* in *sōdan* is composed of the radical for *iu*, "to say," "to talk," on the left and on the right—above and below—the radical for *hi*, "fire" (Fig. 4). Just as a well-laid fire lasts until its purpose has been fulfilled, this kind of talking is apt to go on until all aspects have been explored and a mutually satisfactory solution emerges.

(Go-)sōdan joins with the verb *suru* to mean "to discuss," "to confer," "to consult," all of which are kinds of "reciprocal talking."

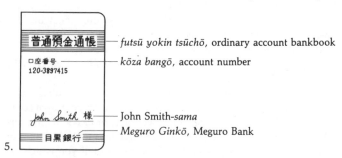

— *futsū yokin tsūchō*, ordinary account bankbook
— *kōza bangō*, account number
— John Smith-*sama*
— *Meguro Ginkō*, Meguro Bank

5.

On opening a bank account, you will receive a bankbook, possibly resembling the one shown in figure 5. The characters on the front tell the type of account and the account number. There is no immediate need to memorize these characters, but for your information *futsū* (seen earlier as indicating a local train) means "ordinary" or "regular"; *yokin* means "bank account," "savings" or "deposit"; and *tsūchō* means "bankbook." You should, however, remember the term *kōza bangō*, "account number," as people who want to transfer money to your account are apt to ask for it.

An account is "ordinary" because deposits and withdrawals can be made freely, even on a daily basis, as is the practice with businesses, large and small. An ordinary account is what most individuals (or families) in this country have instead of a personal checking account, the latter being extraordinarily rare. Although the use of personal checks has never become popular, the country is nonetheless moving from a cash society to a cashless society at about the same pace as other countries, thanks to the diffusion of credit cards, electronic banking programs, personal computers and telecommunication networks, which will soon bring banking into the home.

For the time being you probably still have to go to the bank, so when you want to deposit money look for the window whose specialties include the words in figure 6. Before going to this window you will want to fill in your name, your account number and the amount to be deposited on one of the deposit slips provided. You hand this, with your bankbook and the cash, to the teller. The teller will give you a card with a number on it, so you will want to be ready to hear your number called when the transaction is complete.

6. ご入金 *go-nyūkin*

Go-nyūkin means "honorable money received" (Fig. 6). This *nyū* is the same kanji as in *nyūjōken*, "entrance ticket," and here means "to put in" or "to come in."

The procedure for making a withdrawal is almost identical, except that the withdrawal slip requires your signature or your personal seal in addition to the amount, the account number and your printed name. You will receive a numbered card from the teller, just as when making a deposit. This time it helps insure that your withdrawal is not accidentally given to the wrong person.

7. お引出し *o-hikidashi*　　8. 引 → 引 → 引 *hiki*

The *o* in *o-hikidashi*, literally, "honorable withdrawal" (Fig. 7) is an honorific prefix with exactly the same meaning as *go*. (*Hikidashi* as a form of the verb *hi(ki)da(su)* means "pulling out," from which it got the meaning "drawer.")

The character *hi(ku)* consists of a bow on the left and on the right a straight line to indicate stretching, hence, the idea of "drawing a bow" (Fig. 8). *Hi(ku)* now means "to pull," "to draw" or "to lead." *Da(su)* is a character you have already learned as part of *de-guchi*, "exit" and here it means "to take out" or "to put out," depending perhaps on whether the viewpoint is the banker's or yours.

Banks authorized to deal in foreign exchange frequently have a sign, in English, at the entrance saying "Foreign Exchange." The same sign may be seen at the appropriate teller's window, but if it is a smaller branch bank the only notice may be in Japanese, as shown in figure 9. The same window handles remittances to and from foreign countries.

9. 外国為替 *gaikoku kawase*

Gaikoku kawase means "foreign exchange" (Fig. 9). In *gaikoku*, "foreign country," we have *gai* as in *gaijin*, "foreigner," and *koku* as in *kokusai*, "international."

Kawase, meaning "exchange" or "money order," is an interesting word in that the two kanji used have these pronunciations only in this one word. A common reading of the first character is *tame*, "because of," "as a result of." You should recognize the second character as the *gae* in *ryōgae*, "exchange (of money)."

Three other things about the ordinary account should be mentioned here. When salaries are automatically paid into a bank account on each payday, this is the type of account that usually serves this purpose. Similarly, since personal or even company checks are so rare the ordinary account is a good way to make payments. You can do this by filling out a slip so that the bank will electronically transfer funds from your own account to someone else's. And if you supply anyone with the name of your bank and your personal account number, payments can be made directly into your account—without your ever seeing either money or check! Lastly, ordinary accounts are convenient for paying utility bills, but more about that in the chapter after next.

10. 定期預金 *teiki yokin*

If you plan to live in Japan, you will want to investigate savings plans, the broadest category of which is called *teiki yokin*, "fixed term deposits" (Fig. 10). These are available at the banks where you may have your ordinary account and also at trust banks, which pay higher interest rates. There are several configurations for periods ranging from six months to a decade. The long ones are like pension or annuity plans and, of course, have different names.

This *teiki* is the same compound as in *teiki ken*, commuter pass.

Teiki yokin are among the savings accounts offered at the post office, too. It might be a good idea to compare bank and post office before deciding on long term savings deposits.

24
Bank Machines

Once you have an account at a certain bank, you can apply for a cash card. With your bankbook and/or your cash card and secret ID number, you can deposit or withdraw money from your account by making use of the bank's ATM. This is called *jidō sābisuki*, "automatic service machine." If your only business is to make a withdrawal, there are two more possibilities, *jidō hikidashiki*, an "automatic withdrawal machine," at the bank or *Kasshu Sābisu Kōnā*, a "cash service corner," at a railway station, department store or elsewhere.

1. 自動サービス機
jidō sābisuki

2. 自動引出し機
jidō hikidashiki

As you can see, two of these terms have the *jidō* of *jidō kippu uriba*, "automatic ticket (machines), place of sale." *Hikidashi* (Fig. 2) was discussed in the last chapter and *sābisu* (Fig. 1) means "service."

3. → → 機 *ki*

Here I'd like to add a few words about characters introduced previously but not discussed at that time.

The *ki* in both the foregoing expressions (Fig. 3) is the same as in *hikōki*, "aircraft." With the pronunciation *hata*, it means "loom." This character evolved from meaning a certain part of a loom, to meaning the whole loom and, finally, a "machine." Another meaning of this *ki* is "opportunity."

As you may recall, the money-changing machine in the subway station was simple in design and operation. As befits a financial institution, the bank's money-changing machine is quite sophisticated. It accepts all three denominations of bank notes (¥1,000, ¥5,000, ¥10,000) and gives back smaller bills or coins according to the buttons pushed. Since the operation is an exercise in Arabic numbers, there is no need to explain it here.

4. 両替 *ryōgae*   5. → 両 *ryō*

Ryo, "both," "two," depicts scales of an old-fashioned type, the word for which is *hakari* (Fig. 5). Just as such scales require that the weight on both sides be equal to achieve balance, this kanji forms many compounds where the idea is balance or pairing. Three examples are *ryōte*, "both hands," *ryōashi*, "both feet" and *ryōshin*, "both parents."

The second character in *ryōgae* has the readings *kae(-gae)*, *kae(ru)*, *kawa(ru)*, and *tai* and means "to change" or "to convert." It derives from characters conveying the idea of standing side by side or of different objects appearing alternately.

Now I'd like to go over the instructions necessary to operate the ATM, so that in the future you should be able to use it by yourself. Although machines may differ somewhat from bank to bank, if you know all the key characters you shouldn't have any problems.

The machine used in the example is of the type that both accepts deposits and dispenses money. Since the machines which only pay out money are more simple than this one, I think you will be able to operate them if you know how to use the more complicated one.

The ATM in figure 6 represents schematically the one you will find in your local bank. By matching the numbers in this illustration with the numbered explanations that follow, you should soon become familiar with the basics of this fast and convenient way to do your banking.

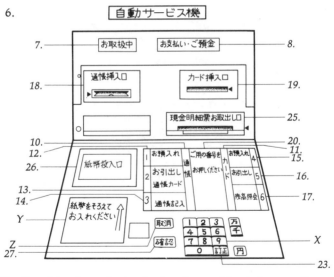

The first thing is to check whether the machine is in operation. Look for the window at the upper left for the kanji in either figure 7A or 7B.

7A. お取扱中 *o-toriatsukaichū*　7B. 使用中止 *shiyō chūshi*

Figure 7A reads *o-toriatsuka(i)chū* and means "in service." If the characters in figure 7B, *shiyō chūshi*, are lit up instead, the machine is out of service at the moment.

8. お支払い・ご預金 *o-shiharai, go-yokin*

The characters in figure 8 say that the machine is programmed and ready for both *o-shiharai*, "(making) payments," and *go-yokin*, "(accepting) deposits."

9. 最初にランプのついているボタンの中から、ご利用の番号をお押しください

Saisho ni ranpu no tsuiteiru botan no naka kara, go-riyō no bangō o o-shi kudasai.

The explanation in figure 9, posted on the wall above the machine, is important because it determines the following step. This, or a similar, message also appears at position 20 and says, "First push the lighted button corresponding to the function you want performed." The first choice is between buttons 1, 2 and 3 in the section numbered 10 and buttons 4, 5 and 6 in the section designated 11.

10. 通帳 *tsūchō*　11. カード *kādo*

Figure 10 shows *tsuchō*, "bankbook"; *kādo* in figure 11 is short for your cash "card." Most systems require that you insert your card as well as your bankbook for withdrawals. Now, time for more choices.

12. お預入れ   13. お引出し   14. 通帳記入
o-azuke ire   *o-hikidashi*   *tsūchō kinyū*

When making a cash deposit using your bankbook only, push button number 1, on which is printed *o-azuke ire*, "making a deposit" (Fig. 12).

When using your bankbook and taking money out of your account, push button number 2, *o-hikidashi*, "withdrawal" (Fig. 13).

If you are not aware of your present balance and simply want your bankbook brought up to date, push button number 3, *tsūchō kinyū*, "bankbook entries" (Fig. 14).

If you are using your card only, the choice is between buttons 4, 5 and 6.

15. お預入れ   16. お引出し   17. 残高照会
o-azuke ire   *o-hikidashi*   *zandaka shōkai*

When you want to make a deposit using your card only, push button number 4, which has printed on it the same words as on button 2 (Fig. 15).

If you want to make a withdrawal using only your card, push button 5 (same as button 2, *o-hikidashi*, Fig. 16).

To get a statement of your current balance using only your card, push button 6. As shown in figure 17 this is called *zandaka shōkai*, "inquiry (as to) balance."

Once you have told the ATM what you want, it will for all practical purposes lead you through the rest of the procedure.

18. 通帳挿入口   19. カード挿入口
tsūchō sōnyū-guchi   *kādo sōnyū-guchi*

If you are using your bankbook, the light at number 18 will blink, indicating where to insert it, namely in the slot under *tsūchō sōnyū-guchi*, literally "bankbook insertion gate" (Fig. 18). Slide your bankbook into this slot, open to the page with the last entry on it. If you are withdrawing money, the ATM will next ask for your card by blinking a light at number 19, *kādo sōnyū-guchi*, "card insertion gate" (Fig. 19). Of course, if you have pushed button 4, 5 or 6, the ATM will ask only for your cash card.

20. 暗証番号をおして下さい

Anshō bangō o oshite kudasai.

The next request will appear as a digital display at position 20. If you are withdrawing money, this will be, "Please push the buttons corresponding to your *anshō bangō*, (secret ID number)" (Fig. 20). The buttons you push for this are the numbered ones at the lower right (position X).

21. 引出すお金をボタンでおします

Hikidasu okane o botan de oshimasu.

22. 3万5千円　¥35,000

Having accepted your bankbook and/or cash card and your secret ID number, the next request appearing at position 20 will be the one shown in figure 21, asking you to "state the amount of money you are withdrawing by pushing the (numbered) buttons (at position X)." The point to be careful about here is that you include the kanji for *man*, *sen* and *en* (buttons to the right of the numbered ones) as shown in figure 22. Otherwise, nothing will happen.

23. 訂正 *teisei*

If by chance you make a mistake in entering the amount, immediately push the button with the word *teisei*, "correction," on it (Fig. 23). Then enter the correct amount.

24. 558,000円までお引出しができます

558,000 en made o-hikidashi ga dekimasu.

Depending on the ATM, the amount which can be withdrawn in one operation may be different. In the case of the machine which we are practicing on, the maximum amount is ¥558,000. The sentence indicating this is given in figure 24. It appears in the general instructions usually found on the wall above the machine. There, too, you will find the capacity of the machine when accepting a single deposit transaction, typically a total of fifty bills of any denomination.

25. 現金明細票お取出し口

genkin meisaihyō o-toridashi-guchi

slot for receiving cash & statement

If you are taking money out of your account, entering the amount is the last step for you. You then wait for the ATM to return your bankbook and cash card and the money you requested, which comes out under the words in figure 25.

26. 紙幣投入口 *shihei tōnyū-guchi*   27. 確認 *kakunin*

Now let's run through the process of depositing money. After you have inserted your bankbook or card, the window labeled *shihei tōnyū-guchi*, "slot for bank notes," will open up like the top of a box (Fig. 26). Lay your deposit, neatly stacked, in the bottom of the receptacle, close the lid, and after a short pause the amount you deposited will appear with the query (at position 20), "Is this correct?" You confirm the amount by pressing the button at 27, on which are the characters *kakunin*, "confirmation" (Fig. 27).

The words at Y and Z are like the notices on automatic ticket vending machines. The instruction at Y is to smooth out bills neatly before you deposit them and Z is the panic button, *torikeshi*, "cancel." Somewhere in the immediate vicinity there is sure to be a *yobidashi* button or, very often, a telephone for the same purpose.

25
Utilities and Taxes

In this chapter we will talk about inevitable things.

People living in apartments or houses discover utility bills in their mailboxes with monotonous regularity. You can take direct action if you like by paying each bill at a bank or post office.

1. 電話料 *denwaryō*   2. 電気料 *denkiryō*

If it is a new experience for you, you can easily locate the right counter by asking, *Denwaryō/denkiryō o haraitai no desu ga, doko no madoguchi desuka*? (Figs. 1–2) ("I want to pay my telephone/electric bill. Which counter is it?")

3. 雨雨 → 雨雨 → 電 *den*   4. 舌 → 話 → 話 *wa*

The first character in both these expressions, *den*, as in *densha*, "electric train," now means "electricity" and at one time had the meaning "lightning" (Fig. 3). It developed as a depiction of rain (the upper half) plus lightning.

The second character in *denwa* is also pronounced *hana(su)* or *hanashi*, "to speak," "to talk" or "conversation" (Fig. 4). It is made up of two radicals: the kanji for *gon, gen, i(u)*, "word" or "to say" on the left and the kanji *shita*, "tongue," on the right. One thing to remember about *denwa* is that it means either "telephone" or "telephone call."

The *ki* of *denki*, "electricity," originally meant "vapor," like that seen rising from boiled rice, and in fact one character for rice was part of this kanji before it was simplified. It has only three pronunciations, *ki*, *ke*, *ge*, but many meanings, including "feeling," "atmosphere," "mind" and "energy," this last being specifically the intrinsic energy of the universe martial artists are always seeking to actualize.

Although the *ryō* in these compounds is the same kanji as in *ryōri*, "cooking," the meaning here is "fee," "charge" rather than "material."

If you prefer not to spend time paying electric, telephone, gas and water bills personally, you can do as the great majority of people in this country do and leave it to the computers. You will first have to inform the bank or post office that you want this done and fill out a form, but then the procedure will become automatic and the appropriate charges will be deducted from your bank or postal savings account, so long as there are sufficient funds in the account.

The rather formidable term for this automatic transfer is given in figure 5.

5. 電気料金領収証 (口座振替払用)
denki ryōkin ryōshūshō (kōza furikae-baraiyō)
recepit (for) electricity charge (by transfer payment [from] account)

Your first look at any utility bill is undoubtedly going to leave you wondering what all those boxes and figures are all about. It would take far too long to explain all of them, so I'll simply give the major points. You can puzzle out the minute details at your leisure.

6. 請求書 *seikyūsho*   7. 領収証 *ryōshūshō*

Postcards are the usual medium for the notices you will receive from the utility companies and your local (ward, city, town or village) water bureau. They fall into two classes, those that can be identified as *seikyūsho*, "bills," and, whatever the method of payment, those that are *ryōshūshō*, "receipts" (Figs. 6–7).

8. 領収金額 *ryōshū kingaku*

The box on the receipt of greatest interest is the one labeled *ryōshū kingaku*, "amount received," sometimes shortened to just *kingaku* (Fig. 8). You can compare this amount with the corresponding entry in your bankbook to see that everything is copacetic.

In figures 9–13 are the full designations for various kinds of receipts and the identity of the senders. I have given the names of the power and gas companies in Tokyo. Residents of other parts of Japan can easily find out the names of the companies in their areas.

Electricity:

9. 電気料金領収証　　　東京電力株式会社
   denki ryōkin ryōshūshō　　*Tōkyō Denryoku Kabushiki-gaisha*
   　　　　　　　　　　　　Tokyo Electric Power Company, Ltd.

Gas:

10. ガス料金領収証　　　東京ガス株式会社
    gasu ryōkin ryōshūshō　　*Tōkyō Gasu Kabushiki-gaisha*
    　　　　　　　　　　　　Tokyo Gas Company, Ltd.

Water:

11. 水道料金領収証　　　水道局
    suidō ryōkin ryōshūshō　　*suidō kyoku*
    　　　　　　　　　　　　water bureau

Telephone:

12. 電信電話料金領収証　　日本電信電話株式会社
    denshin-denwa ryōkin ryōshūshō　　*Nippon Denshin-Denwa Kabushiki-gaisha* Nippon Telegraph & Telephone Corp.

Public broadcasting fee:

13. ＮＨＫ放送受信料領収証　　日本放送協会
    NHK hōsō jushinryō ryōshūshō　　*Nippon Hōsō Kyōkai* Japan Broadcasing Corp.

Salaried employees in Japan have nothing to think about when it comes to paying *zeikin*, "taxes" (Fig. 14). Both the national and local types are deducted from their salaries and paid by their companies directly to the tax offices concerned.

People who are self-employed are responsible for taking care of this matter themselves. The essential point is to file (by March 15) a tax return for the previous calendar year with the national tax office nearest one's residence. (Although the tax form is in Japanese, an instruction pamphlet in English is provided.) The tax office will calculate the taxes due and provide a payment schedule. On the basis of this single return, you will receive a notice of local taxes due from your ward, city, town or village office.

Here again the banks and post offices offer their services. All you have to do is hand over the tax payment slip and cash and the matter will be promptly settled.

14. 税金 *zeikin*   15. 𥝱𦥑 → 𥝱兄 → 税 *zei*

The origin of *zei*, "tax," "duty," is an interesting one (Fig. 15). The left half depicts a rice plant and the right half a person laughing with his mouth wide open. Long ago when taxes were paid with rice, this kanji supposedly referred to the joy evident on the faces of usually stern government officials when the harvest was good and the rice payments flowed in.

Anyway, *zei* combines with *kin*, "money," to make this compound, a word we might like to forget or ignore but won't be allowed to.

26
Body Shops

In the final chapters of this book I will introduce the shops that stock and sell the necessities and some of the frills of everyday life. A glance in the show window will usually tell you immediately what is sold in a particular store, so learning the kanji isn't absolutely necessary. However, being familiar with kanji makes shopping more interesting and meaningful, and if you go to a big department store it would be helpful if you could spot kanji in the store directory. I recommend that you go ahead and learn them.

1. 商店 *shōten*   2. → → 屋 *ya*

Shōten is one word by which "shops" and "stores" are identified (Fig. 1), and there is no end to the number of so-and-so's *shōten* you are likely to come across, for example, *Tanaka shōten*, (Mr.) "Tanaka's shop."

There's more than one way to remember the first character, *shō*, which means "trade" or "merchant." Think of the upper part as being there for the pronunciation. In the lower part can be seen the kanji for *uchi*, "inside," and *kuchi*, "mouth." The idea is to evaluate what is inside (a person) while being able to see only his outside form, as businessmen do when they discuss goods and prices. In Chinese this character refers to the Shang dynasty (eighteenth to twelfth centuries B.C.), which had its capital on a high "plateau," another meaning of the bottom part of the character. As the meaning widened, it came to include peddling, since it appears that the Shang took up itinerant trading after the dissolution of their dynasty. In modern Japanese, this kanji appears in many words having to do with trade, business or commerce.

The second kanji, *ten*, also pronounced *mise*, "shop," has been explained in connection with *kissaten*, "coffee shop." *Ten* is used like a suffix, as you will see in the following pages.

Another word like this is *ya*, "shop," "store," "dealer," also pronounced *oku*, "house" or "roof" (Fig. 2). In the sketch you can see the derivation of this kanji as a picture of a man lying down and a bird stopping on the ground. This came to represent a place to study, rest or live, that is, a house. According to another etymology, the man is sitting and the enclosed part of the character represents an arrow shot at a target, hence a place a man reaches and stays at, i.e., a "house."

Within a particular business field, there may be some preference for *ten* or for *ya*, but in some cases, it can go either way, as in *sho-ten* and *hon-ya*, both meaning "book store."

3. 薬局 *yakkyoku*   薬屋 *kusuriya*

The words for "drugstore," "pharmacy," *yakkyoku* and *kusuriya*, are, in a slightly different way, also a case of either/or (Fig. 3).

The first character in both compounds, *yaku*, means "medicine." With the pronunciation *kusuri*, it means "medicine," "remedy," "enamel" or "benefit."

The *kyoku* in *yakkyoku* is the same as in *yūbin kyoku*, "post office."

4. 化粧品店 *keshōhin ten*   5. → 品 *hin*

Drugstores offer their customers cosmetics as well as medicine, but there are also *keshōhin ten*, "cosmetics shops" (Fig. 4). Nowadays, of course, the products may be for women or men. Competition is keen, and it is one area where both foreign and domestic brands vie to be the sales leader.

Simply giving some of the meanings is all the explanation the first character requires. *Ka*, "influence." *Ke, baka(su)*, "to bewitch." *Bake(ru)*, "to appear in disguise." *Ka(suru)*, "to change," or "to improve."

The next character, *shō*, has the kanji for *kome*, "(uncooked) rice"

137

on the left, and, for pronunciation, the kanji *sho-*, originally meaning "thriving," "flourishing" or "splendid." It represents the idea of "decoration," "ornament." In olden times, women used a white powder ground from rice for makeup.

The third kanji, here pronounced *hin*, is the *shina*, "goods," seen in Shinagawa (Fig. 5).

Here and there you are bound to see the words *keshō shitsu*, but nothing is being sold at these places. The expression is quite the same as the English, "powder room."

6. 美容院 *biyōin*

What would cosmetics be without a visit to your local *biyōin*, "beauty shop" (Fig. 6)? Wherever you go in this country, you will notice that there are an awful lot of beauty salons. This means you definitely have a choice, and you may be treated to a free massage or offered small gifts in addition to hair care.

Bi, "beauty", is the kanji we had in *bijutsukan*, "art museum."

Next comes *yō*, *katachi*, meaning "form," "shape," "appearance." The top part indicates the act of covering up and the bottom has the components seen in the right side of *yoku*, "to bathe."

The idea of the last kanji, *in*, "mansion," "institution," is a building surrounded by an earthen wall, that is, one of particular importance. This character is also part of the word *byōin*, "hospital," so some care in pronunciation is called for. If you do not say these two words distinctly, the next time you ask directions to a beauty shop, you may be sent off in the direction of the hospital.

7. 理髪店 *rihatsu ten*　　理容店 *riyō ten*

Men who want a permanent can go to *rihatsu ten* or *riyō ten*, both of which mean "barbershop," as the sign in front of the shop has it (Fig. 7). Colloquially, you will hear the words *tokoya* and *sanpatsuya* used to refer to the same thing. If your preference is a simple haircut, naturally this is the place for that too, and a shave and a shampoo are included as part of the standard routine.

The *ri*, as seen also in *ryōri*, "cooking," by itself means "reason," "truth" or "principle."

The upper part of *hatsu*, *kami*, "hair," has on the left side one character meaning "long" and three diagonal strokes on the right side representing hair. Long hair was characteristic of women in ancient Japan. The bottom part of this kanji is *tomo*, as seen in *tomodachi*, "friend."

8. ～湯 *yu*　　　せん湯 *sentō*

Anyone wanting to enjoy the roominess and unlimited supply of hot water in the *sentō*, "public bathhouse," had better take advantage of the present situation (Fig. 8). Since dwellings built these days all have their own baths, the number of neighborhood bathhouses has diminished to a fraction of what it once was.

The sign on the front of the public bathhouse may say *sentō*, or it may have the owner's or the local place name plus the character *yu*, "hot water." This kanji has the water radical on the left with the right side providing the pronunciation.

As I mentioned earlier, when *sentō* is written with the kanji for *sen*, it is the character meaning "1/100th of a yen." Believe it or not, in the days of yore, one could wash and soak to his heart's content for this seemingly insignificant sum. It goes without saying that the price is now thousands of times that (currently ¥260), but the pleasure is quite the same.

27
Clothes

Western clothes were extremely rare in Japan prior to the Meiji Restoration, but today they are far and away the most popular wearing apparel.

1. 洋服店 *yōfuku ten*

The shops and department store sections with the sign in figure 1 are the places to look for Western style clothes. It reads, *yōfuku ten* and means "Western clothes shop/store."

This *yō* is the kanji seen in *Taiheiyō,* the "Pacific Ocean," and it is very likely that the linkage between oceans and great distances gave rise to the meaning "Western," as in *Seiyō,* the "Occident," "Europe," and many other words.

The character for *fuku,* "clothes," although it now has the radical for *tsuki,* "moon," on the left, derives from two characters meaning "ship" and to press down on a kneeling person. The whole character once meant a "patch (to repair) a ship," later "to become attached to," and finally "clothes," which are functional only when they are "attached" to a human body.

Depending on who in the family needs a suit or a dress, you can drop in a store displaying one of the three signs in figure 2. *Kodomo* means "child," of course, while *fujin* means "lady," and *shinshi* means "gentleman."

2. 子供服	婦人服	紳士服
kodomo fuku	*fujin fuku*	*shinshi fuku*

Small items like dress shirts, blouses, scarves, socks, handkerchiefs, belts and underwear are sold at *yōhin ten,* literally, "Western goods stores" (Fig. 3).

3. 洋品店 *yōhin ten*

There are no new characters in this compound, so you'll probably be able to recognize it easily enough. A useful word to know at *yōhin ten* is *shitagi,* which means "underwear."

4. 呉服店 *gofuku ten*

The next compound, *gofuku ten,* "kimono shop," may not be a necessary term practically speaking, but if you are interested in

Japanese kimono, it will help you find the shops that sell them (Fig. 4).

The first character in this compound, *go*, *ku(reru)*, "to give," is an interesting one connected with the Wu dynasty in China, but it is not easily analyzable.

Even if you are not planning to buy, just looking at the colors and patterns of kimono in a shop window can be a memorable experience, almost like visiting a museum. Women today prefer elegant jewels, gold and pearls. In days gone by, the hearts of women were filled with joy on receiving a beautiful kimono.

When it is time to replace your shoes or update the style of your footwear, go to the shop with the sign saying *kutsu ten*, "shoe store" (Fig. 5).

5. 靴店 *kutsu ten*

The left side of *kutsu* is one of the kanji meaning *kawa*, "leather." It depicts an animal pelt, without the hair, stretched on a board to dry, that is, in the process of being made into leather. Combined with this on the right side is the character *ka(suru)*, "to change," seen in *keshōhin*, "cosmetics."

28
Some Luxuries

While out shopping have you ever noticed differences between the signs on shops dealing in electrical goods? Although the great majority of shops display the words given in figure 1, those in figures 2 and 3 are not uncommon.

1. 電気店   2. 電機店   3. 電器店
   denki ten   *denki ten*   *denki ten*

Some theoretical differences between these three are possible. For example, *denki ten* (Fig. 1), or *denkiya*, can indicate an "electrician," and as such it would be the place to go if you had an electrical problem to discuss. The *denki* in figure 2 really means "electrical machinery" and is a step away from home appliances. The *denki* in figure 3 is directly translatable as "electric appliances." In practice, the shops under the signs in figures 1 and 3 tend to be pretty much the same—except for the signs.

4. 器 → 器 → 器 *ki*

With one exception, all the characters in these three compounds should be familiar by now.

The kanji in figure 3 pronounced *ki* or *utsuwa*, means "container," "utensil," "instrument" or "apparatus." It consists of elements looking like people and containers and is suggestive of people eating in a group (Fig. 4). This *denki* might be considered a shortening of *denki kigu*, which has the same meaning, "electrical appliance," since the first kanji in the word *kigu* is synonymous with the word itself.

With the right characters in mind, you can go out and get those needed appliances. As with other things, the department store is one possible place and the local retailer is another. For Tokyo residents, there is a third. You may want to drop by Akihabara on the Yamanote Sen. The area close to the station is wholesale outlet after wholesale outlet packed with electrical goods of all descriptions. The discounted prices make for such great bargains that people in other countries have heard of Akihabara and make it one of their stops when they visit Japan. (There is a similar but smaller area in Osaka.)

You don't need to stay in Japan long to learn that the traditional style of living does not call for furniture of the size or type and in the quantities seen in Western homes. Although some Westerners become quite attracted to indigenous furniture, lots of Japanese now have Western style rooms and furniture. For all concerned, the word for "furniture store" is the compound shown in figure 5, *kaguya*.

5. 家具店 *kagu ten*

The *ka* of *kagu* has the same pronunciation as in *kazoku*, "family," the meaning here being "house," "household." The character for *gu*, "tool," "vessel" or "means," comes from a sketch of two hands holding a shell used as a container or tool. (This is the *gu* in *kigu*, mentioned above.)

Clocks and watches may be more like necessities than luxuries. Anyway the place to find them is at the shop with a sign displaying the words in figure 6.

6. 時計店 *tokei ten*

Tokei means "watch," "clock." Its components add up to the meaning, "to measure time."

The *to* in *tokei* is pronounced this way only in this word. It is commonly pronounced *ji*, *toki*, "time," as noted in chapter 6.

The second kanji in *tokei* consists of the radical *gon*, "speech," on the left and on the right, *jū*, specifically "ten" but signifying numbers in general. Pronounced *kei* the whole character means "plan," "stratagem" or "total"; pronounced *haka(ru)* it means "to measure," "to fathom," "to calculate."

When in the buying mood for diamonds, pearls, other jewels or jewelry, look for *hōseki ten*, "jewelry store" (Fig. 7). The Ginza is very well known for, among other things, its many jewelry stores, and even if buying isn't among your immediate plans, it's a great place to window-shop. Many stores have showcases full of costume jewelry in addition to items made of precious stones and metals.

7. 宝石店 *hōseki ten*

The *hō* in *hōseki* is the same kanji is as in *Kokuhō*, "National Treasure." Another pronunciation of this kanji is *takara*, again with the meaning "treasure" or "riches," "wealth."

The second character *seki* was seen in our discussion of *seki-*

tei, "rock garden." Here, of course, the meaning is "stone" rather than "rock."

Probably just as common as the neighborhood appliance store is the local camera shop. Although small, these shops are often photo studios as well as outlets for cameras and photographic equipment and the place to take your film for processing. People who are really into photography–or out to save money–will patronize the discount camera stores which have sprung up in recent years, first in Shinjuku and then in other localities.

These stores are recognizable as either *shashin ten*, "photo shops," or *kamera ten*, "camera stores" (Figs. 8–9). Again it is a case of alternative names for the same type of establishment.

8. 写真店 *shashin ten*   9. カメラ店 *kamera ten*

The first character in *shashin*, *sha*, is also pronounced *utsu(su)* with the meanings "to photograph," "to copy," "to duplicate" or "to reproduce." The top element represents a house and the bottom part is a simplified form of an old character for *kasasagi*, "magpie." Just as the magpie is famous for collecting things by transferring them from one place to another, copying is a process of transferring images.

10. → → 真 *shin*

To get a fix on the second character, *shin*, "truth," "reality," it is best to think upside down, that is, think of an inverted head (Fig. 10). This kanji does in fact come from one depicting a human head upside down. It might be best to imagine a person bowing so low that he is all but standing on his head. Bowing in this fashion is intended to prove that the person is not lying, and thus does the true meaning come to light.

The idea of the two kanji when they are put together in this way to make a compound dovetails very neatly with the English idiom, photographic realism.

29
Some Hobbies

Anytime you are not studying Japanese may be a good time to turn to your favorite sport or hobby, so let's take a first look at those stores.

Music is surely one of the first things to come to mind as a form of recreation. If you want to get a new musical instrument, replace a guitar string or clarinet reed and so on, then *gakki ten*, the "musical instrument store," is the place (Fig. 1).

1. 楽器店 *gakki ten*   2. 𣏟 → 楽 → 楽 *gaku*

Gaku, the first character in this compound, represents a hand-drum on a wooden stand (Fig. 2). The meaning "music" arose from this concrete depiction, and later this kanji acquired the pronunciation *tano(shii)*, "pleasant," "enjoyable," again, no doubt, by association. Yet another pronunciation *raku* means "comfort," "relief." Although I did not mention it at the time, this last meaning is probably the reason this kanji forms the bottom part of the character *kusuri*, "medicine."

This *ki* is the kanji discussed in the last chapter as part of the word *denki*, "electrical appliance."

Jogging is still very much an "in" thing. Besides being good for the health, showing off the latest fashions in training wear plays a part in this popularity. Or at least the prosperity of *supōtsu yōhin ten*, "sporting goods stores," would lead one to think so (Fig. 3). Various kinds of sporting goods are available wherever you go, but if you look around, you will find a shop specializing in the particular field you are interested in, be it skiing, scuba diving or whatever.

3. スポーツ用品店 *supōtsu yōhin ten*

As well as "goods," *yōhin* means "supplies" and is frequently proceeded by a word—such as sports—indicating what kind of goods or supplies are being talked about. The kanji *yō* is very common, meaning "business," "use," "service," or "cost." Added onto a word, it can mean "for the purpose of." You will see it often.

These shops are sometimes referred to as *undōgu ten*, which combines the word *undō*, "exercise," with the *gu* of *kagu* and means roughly "training gear."

Book stores have traditionally handled a wide selection of current books and magazines and little else, but in recent years a few have begun to branch out into minor sidelines. They are identifiable by either of two designations: *hon'ya*, "book store," or *shoten*, "book store" (Fig. 4).

4. 本屋 *hon'ya*　　書店 *shoten*

The kanji *hon* is the same as in *Nihon*, however the meaning in this instance is "book" rather than "main."

The *sho* of *shoten* means "handwriting," "letter," or "book." With the pronunciation *ka(ku)*, it is the common verb "to write." It is composed of elements meaning "hand," "pen" and "various things" and occurs in lots of compounds having to do with published and unpublished documents of various descriptions.

My students of Japanese are always asking me where they can buy stationery and other writing and school supplies. I send them off to *bunbōguya*, the "stationery store" (Fig. 5). Many, I suspect, have a pleasant experience examining the writing implements, papers, drafting instruments and so on carried in a really well-stocked store, for provisions are made not only for writing in the ordinary way but to include the brushes, inkstones and other things necessary for Japanese calligraphy.

5. 文房具屋 *bunbōguya*

The characters are interesting, too. From a long time ago *bun* has been virtually synonymous with Sino-Japanese "writing" and "literature" and is seen in many words like *bunka*, "culture"; *bungaku*, "literature"; and *bungei*, "literary arts."

Bō, "house," "room," is made up of the character for *to*, "door" (top and left), which encloses the second character, which provides the pronunciation. The implication is that where there is a door there is a room. Another word having this kanji is *nyōbō*, "wife," "housewife," "better half," the term by which Japanese men customarily refer to their own spouses.

If your tastes in leisure activities run to making or collecting folk art or handicrafts, the store for you is *mingeihin ten*, literally a "folk art goods shop" (Fig. 6). As you can see, the *mingei* is quite the same as in *mingeikan*, "folk craft museum." Stores of this type are not so plentiful these days, so if you find a particularly good one, you will probably keep going back. The goods available will change, partly because there are seasonal factors and partly because the supply of really hand-crafted objects is often limited.

6. 民芸品店　　7. → 芸 *gei*
  mingeihin ten

As previously noted, *gei*, "art" comes from a depiction of a person planting a tree (Fig. 7). The modern character has at the top the radical *kusa*, "grass," plus an abbreviation of a kanji meaning "to cultivate." Obviously, what's involved is working with the hands and technique, both typical of artists and craftsmen.

Along with works of art, some folk arts and handicrafts become more valuable with age. If you have a sharp eye for these things, the shop is called *kottōhin ten*, "antique/curio shop" (Fig. 8).

8. 骨董品店　　9. → 骨 *kotsu*
  kottōhin ten

Kotsu, hone, the first character in *kottōhin*, means "bone." If we think of how dependent archaeologists often are on ancient skeletons and fragments for information about the past, it's inclusion in this compound seems perfectly natural. *Kotsu* also means "remains."

The meaning of the second kanji is "to manage," "to control." It is not a Jōyō Kanji, so doesn't especially need memorization, but you might want to note that under the upper part, *kusa*, "grass," the rest is the kanji *jū*, *omo(i)*, "weighty," "important." Come to think of it, aren't good antiques sometimes like that, weighty and imposing with their redolence of the past?

You may come across the sign in figure 10 in your search for antiques. Although the meaning of *kobijutsuhin* is the same as *kottōhin*, this term is more likely to be used in writing, while *kottōhin* is more colloquial.

There are certain towns where the chances of finding a choice antique are a bit above the average. Kyoto is one place, of course, as are Takayama in Gifu Prefecture and Kanazawa in Ishikawa Prefecture. In Tokyo, flea markets are held regularly on certain Sundays of each month at Nogi and Tōgō shrines, among other places, and there is a sizable building in Kanda Jinbō-chō, all of whose floors are occupied by antique shops.

10. 古美術品店 *kobijutsuhin ten*

The only new character here is the first one. *Ko*, *furu(i)* means "old." As you can see, this simple character combines the radical for *jū*, "ten," at the top with *kuchi*, "mouth," at the bottom. Attached to this is the idea of oral teaching, from parent to child, for ten generations, certainly a respectable length of time by anyone's reckoning.

Incidentally, if you are looking for a book that is no longer readily available and must try your luck at a used book shop, the word is *furuhon'ya*, "old-book store."

30
Food for Your Table

Previously, we had a look at words having to do with restaurants and dining out. In this chapter, you will find basic characters necessary for people who cook for themselves.

Supermarkets are no novelty in this country, but they must compete with the basement food floors of department stores—patronized by hundreds of shoppers on a typical day—and the traditional distribution system, in which there are a great number of small specialized retailers, some of whom are also makers or processors—located right around the corner.

In better days, the coastal waters of Japan boasted a bountiful supply of fresh fish, a very important source of protein and other nutrients for a country where meat was not part of the diet. Now, due to man's lack of concern during decades of booming industrial growth, the offshore waters are too polluted to yield sufficient catches. Our fishermen have been led into far away international waters, a situation replete with a whole new set of complicated rules, regulations and headaches.

Since meat has become a staple and fish often costs more than meat, fish does not take the precedence it once did. Nevertheless, I think you'll agree that *sashimi*, "raw fish," is still a representative Japanese food. If you want to serve *sashimi* at home, you can start off with a trip to your local *sakanaya*, "fish store" (Fig. 1).

1. 魚屋 *sakanaya*   2. 🐟 → 奥 → 魚 *sakana*

There is not too much to say about the kanji *sakana*, "fish," other than that it is based on a sketch of a fish (Fig. 2). It has two other readings, *gyo* and *uo*, but no other meanings. Not surprisingly, it is seen in the names of scores of fishes. (*See* chapter 19.)

On those days when you prefer meat to fish, you can stop by the *nikuya*, "meat shop" (Fig. 3). The standard offerings are beef, pork and chicken, in several grades and cuts. You can make your selections as your eye sees fit and—especially if it is beef—in consultation with your pocketbook.

3. 肉屋 *nikuya*　4. 牛乳屋 *gyūnyūya*

The kanji for *niku* and *gyū*, "cow," were presented in the chapter on restaurants, but while we're on the subject of cows is a good time to find out about *gyūnyūya*, the "milk store" (Fig. 4).

The second character in this compound, *nyū*, *chichi*, means "milk" or "breasts." The significant part to remember is at the lower left where you can see the character *shi*, meaning "child." (*See* chapter 18.)

Home delivery of milk is generally available from your neighborhood *gyūnyūya*. Moreover, milk is looked upon as a refreshing drink, or perhaps it is good for stamina, and as such is sold in small bottles or cartons at kiosks in train stations, for example, and in vending machines. Sometimes you will have a choice between cold and warm milk drinks.

A store selling meat is a *nikuya* and a store selling fish is a *sakanaya*, so why isn't a shop selling *yasai*, "vegetables," called a *yasaiya*? Well, that is a mystery to unravel. The actual term is *yaoya*, "vegetable store," "green grocer" (Fig. 5) and the word *yasaiya* does not exist.

5. 八百屋 *yaoya*　6. → ノ ＼ → 八 *ya*

Even Japanese children have to learn that this compound is not pronounced as *happyaku*, "800," plus *ya*, but why this is so deserves a little speculation.

With its four seasons, moderate climate and ample rainfall

Japan is a country where things grow fast and well, especially with the aid of agricultural techniques perfected over many hundreds of years. The result is not 800 varieties of vegetables literally speaking, but we should nevertheless accept *hachi, ya,* "8," as a lucky number (Fig. 6). One reason for this is that on each hand there are 4 fingers, total: 8. And when 2 is cubed, the result is 8, in other words 8 is the only single digit whose cube root is a whole number. Because of this, the number 8 is much sought after in business phone numbers. Then, too, it represents the advance of time. With their many kinds of vegetables, the owners of these shops hope to advance into a profitable future. This is seen in the middle of figure 6 by the way both sides of the kanji *ya* spread out gradually, like an arrow pointing forward.

As for the second kanji, there seem to be few other cases where *o* is substituted for *hyaku*, but that is the situation we have here. It is just one of those words that has to be remembered as it is.

In what might be regarded as a breach of tradition, or merely economic sense, *yaoya* sell fruits as well as vegetables. But that doesn't mean there aren't shops handling fruit only. These go by the name of *kudamonoya*, "fruit stores" (Fig. 7).

7. 果物屋 *kudamonoya*   8. → 果 → 果 *kuda*

A long time ago, someone drew a picture to conjure up the image of a fruit-laden tree, and this was to become the basis for the character *kuda* (Fig. 8) in *kudamono,* "fruit." More usual pronunciations of this kanji are *ha(tasu),* "to achieve," "to complete," and *ka* in such words as *kajū,* "fruit juice," and *kōka,* "effect," "efficacy." The appropriateness is obvious, since fruit bearing takes place on mature trees, at the last stage of a growth cycle.

The *mono* in *kudamono* is the same kanji as *butsu* in *hakubutsukan.*

Fruit is important, too, to confectioners, who operate under the *kashiya* sign shown in figure 9. *Kashi* is a very broad category of comestibles, and the term may be heard with reference to everything from Western cakes, cookies and biscuits through a

151

multitude of Japanese sweets to the crackers made from rice flour and known as *o-senbe*, of which there is also a very wide selection. To make things slightly easier, the whole array is divided into *yō-gashi*, "Western" *kashi* and *wa-gashi*, "Japanese" *kashi*.

9. 菓子屋 *kashiya*

As you can see, the kanji for *ka*, "cake," "fruit," is written with the character *ka*, "fruit," and *kusa*, "grass," at the top. It is said that from the time they were invented, fruits were a major ingredient of Chinese sweets and this is still true today.

The second character, read *shi* or *ko*, is the *ko* of *kodomo*, "child." (Remember *kodomo fuku* in chapter 27?) Needless to say, children are extremely fond of sweets, but the inclusion of this kanji in this compound may have more to do with another meaning of *shi*, namely, "fruit" or "seed."

All food and no drink is not an ideal situation. For potables to complement a meal, drop by the *sakaya*, "liquor store," nearest you, or telephone and have what you want delivered (Fig. 10). Since the system is free enterprise, any particular store's inventory may lean more heavily towards Western spirits or the indigenous *Nihonshu* and *shochū*. If you shop around you should be able to find almost anything you want.

10. 酒屋 *sakaya*

The kanji for *sake* came up before in chapter 20. Here we might observe that from the point of view of materials and method of fermentation, it should probably be called "rice beer" rather than the traditional "rice wine." But never mind. On the average, it is about three or four times more potent than beer, and the ways of packaging, serving and drinking it are more befitting a wine than a beer. One of the great surprises in store for the newcomer is the great number of different types of *Nihonshu*. Sake tasting can be every bit as challenging as wine tasting. Enjoyable, too.

I will close on a general, non-specialized note. The compound in figure 11 reads *shokuryōhin ten* and is generally equivalent to "grocery store." What you can expect to find here are basics like salt and other condiments, canned goods and other prepared and packaged foods and so on. If a store goes beyond this and includes such things as a meat counter or fruit and vegetables, etc., it will probably call itself *sūpā*, as in *sūpāmāketto*, i.e., "supermarket," or some variation thereof.

11. 食料品店 *shokuryōhin ten*

The three characters in *shokuryōhin*, "foodstuffs," "provisions," "groceries," are *shoku* as in *shokudō*, "restaurant"; *ryō* as in *ryōri*, "cuisine"; and *hin* as in *keshōhin*, "cosmetics."

Appendix: Vocabulary Building

1: STATIONS AND TRAINS

駅　*eki*

駅 弁　*ekiben*, station (box) lunch
駅 長　*ekichō*, station master
駅 員　*ekiin*, station employee
駅 前　*ekimae*, (area) in front of station

口　*kuchi/-guchi*

非 常 口　*hijō-guchi*, emergency exit

入　*nyū, i(ri)*

入 院　*nyūin*, hospitalization
入 国　*nyūkoku*, entering a country

出　*de, shutsu*

出来立て　*dekitate*, fresh, just made
出 発　*shuppatsu*, departure
出 席　*shusseki*, attendance

札　*satsu*

札 束　*satsutaba*, roll of bank notes

東　*tō, higashi*

東 北　*tōhoku, higashikita*, northeast

東 南　*tōnan, higashiminami*, southeast
東 洋　*Tōyō*, the Orient

南　*nan, minami*

南 北　*nanboku*, north-south
南 西　*nansei, minaminishi*, southwest

北　*hoku, kita*

北 西　*hokusei, kitanishi*, northwest

西　*sei, nishi*

西 部　*seibu*, western part
西 北　*seihoku*, northwest
大 西 洋　*Taiseiyō*, Atlantic Ocean

中　*chū, naka*

中 部　*chūbu*, central part
中 学 校　*chūgakkō*, middle school
中 近 東　*Chūkintō*, Middle East
中 心　*chūshin*, center, middle

目　*moku, me*

目 上　*meue*, superior
目覚時計　*mezamashi-dokei*, alarm clock

見		*ken, mi(ru), mi(seru)*
見	物	*kenbutsu*, sightseeing
見	本	*mihon*, sample
左		*sa, hidari*
左	手	*hidari te*, left hand
左	派	*saha*, left wing
右		*u, migi*
右	手	*migi te*, right hand
右	派	*uha*, right wing
山		*san, yama*
山	頂	*sanchō*, mountain top
山	脈	*sanmyaku*, mountain range
外		*gai, ge, soto, hoka*
外	国	*gaikoku*, foreign country
外出中		*gaishutsuchū*, be out (of the office)
外	科	*geka*, surgery
内		*nai, uchi*
内	閣	*naikaku*, cabinet
内線番号		*naisen bangō*, extension number
方		*hō, kata*
方	法	*hōhō*, method, way
方		*. . . kata*, c/o, in care of
新		*shin, atara(shii)*
新	聞	*shinbun*, newspaper
新学期		*shingakki*, new school term
新発売		*shinhatsubai*, new product/model
新	館	*shinkan*, annex

新	年	*shinnen*, New Year
新	鮮	*shinsen*, fresh
上		*jō, ue, kami, nobo(ri)*
上	品	*jōhin*, elegance
上	旬	*jōjun*, first third of month
上	級	*jōkyū*, high grade
上	手	*jōzu*, skillful
線		*sen*
線	香	*senkō*, incense stick
線	路	*senro*, railroad track
国		*koku, kuni*
国	道	*kokudō*, national highway
国	内	*kokunai*, domestic
国	連	*Kokuren*, U.N.
下		*ka, ge, shita, shimo*
下	旬	*gejun*, last third of month
下	車	*gesha*, getting off (bus, train)
下	水	*gesui*, drainage
下	手	*heta*, unskillful
下	着	*shitagi*, underwear
車		*sha, kuruma*
車	庫	*shako*, car barns
車	内	*shanai*, inside a vehicle
車	掌	*shashō*, conductor
列	車	*ressha*, train
行		*kō, yu(ki), i(ku)*
行き止まり		*yuki-domari*, no passage, dead end
行き先		*yukisaki*, destination, address

急　　*kyū, iso(gu)*

急 場　*kyūba*, emergency
急 病　*kyūbyō*, sudden illness
急 停 車　*kyūteisha*, sudden
　　stop

男　　*dan, otoko*

男 性　*dansei*, male
男 子　*danshi*, men
男 の 子　*otoko no ko*, boy

女　　*jo, nyō, onna*

女 性　*josei*, female
女 子　*joshi*, women
女 房　*nyōbō*, wife
女 の 子　*onna no ko*, girl

精　　*sei*

精（白）米　*sei(haku)mai*, pol-
　　ished rice
精 肉　*seiniku*, fresh meat
精 神　*seishin*, spirit

2: TICKET MACHINES, TRAINS

自　　*ji, shi*

自 宅　*jitaku*, one's home
自 転 車　*jitensha*, bicycle
自 然　*shizen*, nature

動　　*dō, ugo(ku)*

動 物　*dōbutsu*, animal
動 物 園　*dōbutsuen*, zoo
動 機　*dōki*, motive
運 動　*undō*, movement

近　　*kin, chika(i)*

近 道　*chikamichi*, short cut
近 所　*kinjo*, neighborhood

投　　*tō, nage(ru)*

投 票　*tōhyō*, voting

投 手　*tōshu*, pitcher

金　　*kin, kane, kana*

金 物　*kanamono*, hardware
金 槌　*kanazuchi*, hammer
金 融　*kin'yū*, finance
金 曜 日　*kin'yōbi*, Friday
金 属　*kinzoku*, metal
貴 金 属　*kikinzoku*, precious
　　metal

人　　*jin, nin, hito*

人 々　*hitobito*, people
人 口　*jinkō*, population
人 差 指　*hitosashiyubi*, index
　　finger
人 間　*ningen*, human being
人 形　*ningyō*, doll

3: TICKET MACHINES, SUBWAYS

営　　*ei, itona(mu)*

経 営　*keiei*, management

団　　*dan, ton*

団 地　*danchi*, housing com-
　　plex
団 体　*dantai*, body, group
蒲 団　*futon*, mattress, quilt

全　　*zen*

全 部　*zenbu*, all, the whole
全 員　*zen'in*, all employees
全 国　*zenkoku*, the whole
　　country
全 力　*zenryoku*, all-out effort
全 勝　*zenshō*, straight wins

都　　*to*

都 知 事　*tochiji*, metropolitan

governor

都 庁　*tochō*, metropolitan office

都 民　*tomin*, citizens of Tokyo

都 内　*tonai*, within the capital

都 立　*toritsu*, metropolitan

都 心　*toshin*, center of metropolis

両　*ryō*

両 足　*ryōashi*, both feet

両 方　*ryōhō*, both

両 面　*ryōmen*, both surfaces

4: STATION WINDOWS

定　*tei*

定 義　*teigi*, definition

定 員　*teiin*, regular staff

定 刻　*teikoku*, appointed time

定 価　*teika*, established price

決 定　*kettei*, conclusion

期　*ki*

期 限　*kigen*, time limit

期 間　*kikan*, term, period

期 末　*kimatsu*, end of term

券　*ken*

整 理 券　*seiriken*, (fare) adjustment ticket

商 品 券　*shōhinken*, gift certificate

招 待 券　*shōtaiken*, invitation card

回　*kai, mawa(ri)*

回 復　*kaifuku*, recovery

回 覧 板　*kairanban*, circular notice

回 答　*kaitō*, answer

回 り 舞 台　*mawaributai*, revolving stage

回 り 道　*mawarimichi*, detour

指　*shi, yubi*

指 圧　*shiatsu*, finger pressure (massage/therapy)

指 示　*shiji*, instructions

指 先　*yubisaki*, fingertip

忘　*bō, wasu(reru)*

忘 れ 物　*wasuremono*, forgotten article

忘 年 会　*bōnenkai*, year-end party

5: TAXIS

大　*tai, dai, ō, ō(kii), ō-(kisa)*

大 学　*daigaku*, college, university

大 臣　*daijin*, minister

大 小　*daishō*, large and small

大 統 領　*daitōryō*, president

大 瓶　*ōbin*, large bottle

大 家　*ōya*, landlord

大 会　*taikai*, large meeting, tournament

大 使 館　*taishikan*, embassy

大 衆　*taishū*, general public

小　*ko, shō, chii(sai)*

小 瓶　*kobin*, small bottle

小 麦 粉　*komugiko*, wheat flour

小 指　*koyubi*, little finger

小 学 校　*shōgakkō*, elementary school

個　*ko*

個 人 的　*kojinteki*, personal

個 性 *kosei*, individuality

6: BUSES

日 *jitsu, nichi, hi/-bi*

日 米 *Nichi-Bei*, Japan-U.S.
日 英 *Nichi-Ei*, Japan-England
日 濠 *Nichi-Gō*, Japan-Australia
日 時 *nichiji*, date and time
日 常 *nichijō*, everyday
日 曜 日 *nichiyōbi*, Sunday
日本銀行 *Nihon Ginkō*, Bank of Japan
日 本 語 *Nihongo*, Japanese
日 本 人 *Nihonjin*, Japanese
日 加 *Nik-Ka*, Japan-Canada
日 中 *Nit-Chū*, Japan-China
平 日 *heijitsu*, weekday
祝 日 *shukujitsu*, red-letter day
毎 日 *mainichi*, every day

時 *ji, toki*

時 間 *jikan*, hour, time
時 刻 表 *jikokuhyō*, timetable
時 差 *jisa*, time difference
同 時 *dōji*, (at the) same time

休 *kyū, yasu(mu)*

休 日 *kyūjitsu*, holiday
休 暇 *kyūka*, holiday, day off
休 憩 *kyūkei*, recess

7: AIRPORTS

際 *sai*

実 際 *jissai*, actuality

空 *kū, a(ki), sora*

空き部屋 *akibeya*, vacant room
空 き 瓶 *akibin*, empty bottle
空 き 罐 *akikan*, empty can
空 気 *kūki*, air, atmosphere
空 室 *kūshitsu*, vacant room

成 *sei, na(ru)*

成人の日 *seijin no hi*, Adult's Day
成 績 *seiseki*, record

田 *den, ta*

田 舎 *inaka*, rural areas
田 ん ぼ *tanbo*, rice paddy

港 *kō, minato*

漁 港 *gyokō*, fishing port

航 *kō*

航海する *kōkai suru*, to sail
航行する *kōkō suru*, to cruise
欠 航 *kekkō*, suspension of service
日本航空 *Nihon Kōkū*, Japan Air Lines

飛 *hi, to(bu)*

飛び出す *tobidasu*, rush out, appear (suddenly)

8: INNS

交 *kō*

交 番 *kōban*, police box
交 差 点 *kōsaten*, intersection
交 代 (替) *kōtai*, alternation
交通安全 *kōtsū anzen*, traffic safety
交通事故 *kōtsū jiko*, traffic accident
交通信号 *kōtsū shingō*, traffic signal

通　　*tsū, tō(ru)*

通 学　*tsūgaku*, going to school

通 過 駅　*tsūka eki*, train-doesn't-stop station

通 行　*tsūkō*, passage

通 行 止　*tsūkō-dome*, suspension of traffic

通用期間　*tsūyō kikan*, period of validity

公　　*kō, ōyake*

公 演　*kōen*, public performance

公 害　*kōgai*, pollution

公 開　*kōkai*, open to public

公共料金　*kōkyō ryōkin*, public utilities charges

公 立　*kōritsu*, public

公衆電話　*kōshū denwa*, public telephone

社　　*sha*

社 長　*shachō*, company president

社 員　*shain*, (regular) company employee

社 会　*shakai*, society

出 社　*shussha*, present at the office

旅　　*ryo, tabi*

旅 客　*ryokaku*, tourist, passenger

会　　*kai/-gai, a(u)*

会 長　*kaichō*, chairman

会 談　*kaidan*, conference

会 議 中　*kaigichū*, in conference

会 員　*kaiin*, society member

会 場　*kaijō*, meeting place

会 館　*kaikan*, hall

会 計　*kaikei*, bill

会 話　*kaiwa*, conversation

観　　*kan*

観 光 団　*kankōdan*, tourist party

観 光 客　*kankōkyaku*, tourist

案　　*an*

案 内　*annai*, guidance

案 内 図　*annaizu*, guide map

館　　*kan*

映 画 館　*eigakan*, movie house

図 書 館　*toshokan*, library

民　　*min*

民 間　*minkan*, private, civilian

民 謡　*min'yō*, folk song

宿　　*shuku/-juku, yado*

宿 場　*shukuba*, inn town

宿 舎　*shukusha*, lodging house

合 宿　*gasshuku*, boarding house

9: ONE NIGHT, TWO MEALS

泊　　*haku/-paku, toma(ru)*

外 泊　*gaihaku*, spending the night outside (one's home)

食　　*shoku, ta(beru)*

食べ放題　*tabehōdai*, eat until full

食 後　*shokugo*, after a meal

食 品 *shokuhin*, foodstuffs
食 事 *shokuji*, meal
食 糧 *shokuryō*, main diet
食 用 *shokuyō*, edible
食 物 *tabemono, shoku-motsu*, food

付 *fu, tsu(ku), tsu(ki), tsu(keru)*

付 属 *fuzoku*, affiliated

料 *ryō*

給 料 *kyūryō*, salary
有 料 *yūryō*, toll
材 料 *zairyō*, material

予 *yo*

予防注射 *yobō chūsha*, immunization
予 報 *yohō*, forecast
予 算 *yosan*, budget

約 *yaku*

約 束 *yakusoku*, promise
契 約 *keiyaku*, contract

10: BATHS

洗 *sen, ara(u)*

洗 面 器 *senmenki*, wash basin
洗 濯 *sentaku*, washing
洗 濯 機 *sentakuki*, washing machine
洗 剤 *senzai*, detergent

面 *men, omote*

面 *men*, mask
面 会 *menkai*, interview
面 積 *menseki*, area

所 *jo, sho, tokoro*

所 帯 主 *shotai nushi*, head of household
所 得 *shotoku*, income
所 得 税 *shotokuzei*, income tax
所 在 *shozai*, whereabouts
停 留 所 *teiryūjo*, (bus/tram) stop
区 役 所 *kuyakusho*, ward office
市 役 所 *shiyakusho*, city office

室 *shitsu*

室 温 *shitsuon*, room temperature

場 *jō, ba*

場 所 *basho*, place, location
場 内 *jōnai*, on the grounds

家 *ka, ke, ya, ie*

家 主 *yanushi*, house owner
家 庭 *katei*, household
家 賃 *yachin*, rent

風 *fu/bu, fū, kaze*

風 呂 釜 *furogama*, bath heater
風 呂 場 *furoba*, bathroom
風 呂 桶 *furo oke*, bathtub
風 流 *fūryū*, refinement
風 速 *fūsoku*, wind speed
風 雨 *fūu*, wind and rain
台 風 *taifū*, typhoon

11: NATURAL FEATURES

川 *sen, kawa/-gawa*

川 岸 *kawagishi*, riverbank

木　　*moku, ki*

木 版 画　*mokuhanga*, wood-
　　　block print
木 製 品　*mokuseihin*, wood
　　　products
木 曜 日　*mokuyōbi*, Thursday
木 造　*mokuzō*, wooden

立　　*ritsu, ta(tsu), tachi*

立 場　*tachiba*, standpoint
立入り禁止　*tachiiri kinshi*, en-
　　　trance prohibited

温　　*on, atata(kai)*

温 度　*ondo*, temperature
温 度 計　*ondokei*, thermo-
　　　meter

湖　　*ko, mizuumi*

湖 畔　*kohan*, lakeshore

海　　*kai, umi*

海 老　*ebi*, shrimp
海 外　*kaigai*, overseas
海 上　*kaijō*, maritime
海 峡　*kaikyō*, channel
瀬戸内海　*Setonai Kai*

島　　*tō, shima/-jima*

島 国　*shimaguni*, island
　　　country
半 島　*hantō*, peninsula

12: SHINTŌ AND BUDDHISM

神　　*shin, jin, kami*

神 風　*kamikaze*, divine wind
神 主　*kannushi*, Shintō priest
神 仏　*shinbutsu*, gods and
　　　Buddhas
神 経　*shinkei*, nerve

神 秘　*shinpi*, mystery

道　　*dō, michi*

道 具　*dōgu*, tool, instrument
道 場　*dōjō*, training hall
道 路　*dōro*, road, route
道 徳　*dōtoku*, morals

宮　　*gū, ku, miya*

宮 司　*gūji*, chief priest
　　　(Shintō)
宮 参 り　*miyamairi*, shrine
　　　visit

仏　　*Butsu, Futsu, Hotoke*

仏 壇　*Butsudan*, Buddhist
　　　(household) altar
仏　　*Futsu*, French
大 仏　*Daibutsu*, Great Bud-
　　　dha (statue)

寺　　*ji, tera/-dera*

寺 町　*teramachi*, temple town

13: STATUE AND GARDEN

宝　　*hō, takara*

宝 庫　*hōko*, treasure house
宝 物　*hōmotsu, takaramono*,
　　　treasure
宝 舟　*takara-bune*, treasure
　　　ship

拝　　*hai(suru)*

拝 啓　*haikei*, Dear Sir/Ma-
　　　dame
参 拝　*sanpai*, worship

石　　*seki, ishi*

石 垣　*ishigaki*, stone wall

石 仏 *seki Butsu*, stone Buddha (statue)
石 油 *sekiyu*, kerosene, petroleum
石 鹸 *sekken*, soap

14: CASTLES AND MUSEUMS

城 *jō, shiro*

城 下 *jōka*, castle town
城 跡 *shiro ato*, castle ruins/site

江 *e*

江戸前鮨 *Edomae-zushi*

皇 *kō*

皇 女 *kōjo, ōjo*, imperial princess
皇 后 *kōgō*, empress
皇 子 *kōshi, ōji*, imperial prince
皇 室 *Kōshitsu*, Imperial Household
皇 太 子 *kōtaishi*, crown prince

居 *kyo, i(ru), o(ru)*

居 所 *idokoro*, whereabouts, address
居 酒 屋 *izakaya*, pub
居 住 地 *kyojūchi*, address

美 *bi, utsuku(shii)*

美 男 子 *bidanshi/binanshi*, handsome man
美 人 *bijin*, beautiful woman
美 術 品 *bijutsuhin*, work of art

博 *haku/-baku/-paku*

博 打 *bakuchi*, gambling

博 学 *hakugaku*, erudition
博 覧 会 *hakurankai*, exposition
博 士 *hakase/hakushi*, Ph.D.

物 *butsu, mono*

物 価 *bukka*, prices
物 品 *buppin*, goods, articles
物 産 *bussan*, product
物 語 *monogatari*, story
物 置 *monooki*, storage room
物差し(指し) *monosashi*, ruler

芸 *gei*

芸 術 *geijutsu*, art
芸 術 家 *geijutsuka*, artist
芸 名 *geimei*, stage name
芸 能 人 *geinōjin*, performer
芸 者 *geisha*, geisha

展 *ten*

展 望 台 *tenbōdai*, observatory
展 示 *tenji*, display

15: GEOGRAPHY

本 *hon/-pon/-bon*

本 部 *honbu*, headquarters
本 堂 *hondō*, main (temple) hall
本 日 *honjitsu*, today
本 館 *honkan*, main building
本 局 *honkyoku*, main office
本 人 *honnin*, the person himself
本 線 *honsen*, main line
本 社 *honsha*, main company
本 店 *honten*, head office

太 *tai, futo(i)*

太 陽 *taiyō*, sun

平　　*hei, byō, tai(ra), hira*

平方メートル　*heihō mētoru,* square meter

平　常　*heijō,* normal, usual
平　気　*heiki,* composure
平　均　*heikin,* average
平　仮　名　*hiragana*

洋　　*yō*

洋　風　*yōfū,* Western style
洋　画　*yōga,* Western painting/film
洋　菓　子　*yō-gashi,* Western confectionery
洋　式　*yōshiki,* Western style
洋　室　*yōshitsu,* Western-style room
洋　書　*yōsho,* Western books
洋　食　*yōshoku,* Western food
洋　酒　*yōshu,* Western liquor

16: NUMBERS

百　　*hyaku*

百　貨　店　*hyakka ten,* department store

万　　*man, ban*

万　国　*bankoku,* all nations
万　博　*banpaku,* international exposition
万　歳　*banzai,* hurrah

億　　*oku,* 100,000,000

兆　　*chō,* 1,000,000,000,000

17: NOODLES

理　　*ri*

理　事　長　*rijichō,* board chairman

理　由　*riyū,* reason, cause

冷　　*rei, hiya(shi)*

冷　麦　*hiyamugi,* cold noodles
冷　奴　*hiyayakko,* cold tofu
冷　酒　*hiyazake,* cold sake
冷　房　*reibō,* air conditioning
冷　凍　*reitō,* refrigeration
冷　蔵　庫　*reizōko,* refrigerator

打　　*da, u(tsu)*

打　者　*dasha,* batter

焼　　*shō, ya(ku)*

焼　酎　*shōchū,* a liquor
焼　き　豚　*yakibuta,* roast pork
焼　き　芋　*yakiimo,* roasted sweet potato
焼　き　飯　*yakimeshi,* fried rice
焼　き　物　*yakimono,* pottery
焼　き　肉　*yakiniku,* roasted meat
焼き立て　*yakitate,* fresh made
焼　き　魚　*yaki-zakana,* broiled fish
鍋　焼　*nabeyaki,* pot boiled

味　　*mi, aji*

味　付　け　*ajitsuke,* seasoning
味　方　*mikata,* ally

18: RESTAURANT AND *SHOKUDŌ*

天　　*ten*

天　国　*tengoku,* paradise
天　井　*tenjō,* ceiling
天　気　*tenki,* weather
天皇陛下　*Tennō Heika,* His Majesty the Emperor

親　　*shin, oya, shita(shii)*

親　指　*oyayubi,* thumb

親 戚 *shinseki*, relative
親 展 *shinten*, confidential
親 友 *shin'yū*, close friend

子 *shi, ko/-go*

子 牛 *koushi*, calf
子 女 *shijo*, children
子 孫 *shison*, descendant
妻 子 *saishi*, wife and children

玉 *tama/-dama*

玉 葱 *tamanegi*, onion

19: GRILLED CHICKEN AND RAW FISH

鳥 *chō, tori*

鳥 肉 *toriniku*, poultry meat

司 *shi*

司 書 *shisho*, librarian

20: A GLASSFUL, A BOTTLE

酒 *shu, sake/-zake*

酒 場 *sakaba*, bar
酒 屋 *sakaya*, liquor store
酒 造 *shuzō*, sake brewing
地 酒 *jizake*, local sake

生 *sei, shō, ki-, nama, i-(kiru), u(mare), na(ru)*

生 花 *ikebana*, flower arrangement
生 地 *kiji*, cloth
生 野 菜 *nama yasai*, raw vegetables
生 魚 *nama-zakana*, raw fish
生 活 *seikatsu*, life, livelihood
生命保険· *seimei hoken*, life insurance

生年月日 *seinengappi*, date of birth
生 徒 *seito*, pupil
学 生 *gakusei*, student
先 生 *sensei*, teacher
誕 生 日 *tanjōbi*, birthday

21: OPEN FOR BUSINESS

茶 *sa, cha*

茶 道 *sadō*, Way of Tea
茶 菓 子 *cha-gashi*, tea cakes
茶 会 *chakai*, tea party
茶 色 *chairo*, brown
茶 の 湯 *chanoyu*, tea ceremony
茶 室 *chashitsu*, tearoom
茶 碗 *chawan*, tea bowl
茶 漬 *chazuke*, tea and rice mixed

弁 *ben(zuru)*

弁 護 士 *bengoshi*, lawyer
弁 天 *Benten*, god of wealth

当 *tō*

当 駅 *tōeki*, this station
当 時 *tōji*, at that time
当 選 *tōsen*, election

業 *gyō, waza*

業 務 *gyōmu*, business, affairs, operations
企 業 *kigyō*, enterprise
工 業 *kōgyō*, manufacturing
農 業 *nōgyō*, agriculture
産 業 *sangyō*, industry
商 業 *shōgyō*, commerce

備 *bi, sona(eru)*

備 蓄 *bichiku*, emergency stores

終　　*shū, owa(ru)*

終電車　*shūdensha*, last train
終点　*shūten* last stop

了　　*ryō*

了承　*ryōshō*, acknowledgment
了解　*ryōkai*, understanding

売　　*bai, u(ru)*

売買　*baibai*, buying and selling
売店　*baiten*, stand
売り上げ　*uriage*, amount of sales
売り出し　*uridashi*, (bargain) sale
発売中　*hatsubaichū*, now on sale

22: POST OFFICE

京　　*kyō*

京風　*kyōfū*, Kyoto style
京阪　*Kei-Han*, Kyoto-Osaka
京阪神　*Kei-Han-Shin*, Kyoto-Osaka-Kobe
京浜　*Kei-Hin*, Tokyo-Yokohama

他　　*ta*

他方　*tahō*, another side

府　　*fu*

府知事　*fuchiji*, prefectural governor
府庁　*fuchō*, prefectural office
府立　*furitsu*, prefectural

県　　*ken*

県知事　*ken chiji*, prefectural governor

県庁　*kenchō*, prefectural office
県道　*kendō*, prefectural road
県立　*kenritsu*, prefectural

郵　　*yū*

郵便貯金　*yūbin chokin*, postal savings
郵便為替　*yūbin kawase*, postal money order
郵便私書箱　*yūbin shisho-bako*, post office box
郵便屋　*yūbinya*, postman

便　　*bin, ben*

便利な　*benri na*, convenient

切　　*ki(ru), ki(reru)*

切符　*kippu*, ticket
切り身　*kirimi*, slice, cut (meat, fish)

包　　*hō, tsutsu(mu), tsutsu-(mi)/-zutsu(mi)*

包丁　*hōchō*, kitchen knife
包帯　*hōtai*, roll bandage
包み紙　*tsutsumigami*, wrapping paper

23: BASICS OF BANKING

相　　*sō, ai*

相手　*aite*, companion, opponent
相互銀行　*sōgo ginkō*, mutual savings and loan bank
相撲　*sumō*, sumo

談　　*dan*

談義　*dangi*, lecture

引　　*hiki*

引 手　*hikite*, knob, handle
引 越　*hikkoshi*, house moving

24: BANK MACHINES

機　　*ki, hata*

機 長　*kichō*, pilot
機 会　*kikai*, opportunity
機 内　*kinai*, inside the plane

25: UTILITIES AND TAXES

電　　*den*

電 池　*denchi*, battery
電気剃刀　*denki kamisori*, electric razor
電 気 工　*denkikō*, electrician
電 報　*denpō*, telegram
電 線　*densen*, electric line
電 信　*denshin*, telegraph
電 送　*densō*, facsimile transmission
電 鉄　*dentetsu*, electric railway
電 灯　*dentō*, electric light
電 話 機　*denwaki*, telephone (instrument)

話　　*wa, hana(su), hanashi/-banashi*

話 題　*wadai*, topic of conversation
昔 話　*mukashi-banashi*, legend, folklore

税　　*zei*

税 額　*zeigaku*, tax amount
税 関　*zeikan*, customs (house)
税 務 署　*zeimusho*, tax office

26: BODY SHOPS

商　　*shō*

商 売　*shōbai*, business, occupation
商 品　*shōhin*, goods, merchandise
商 工 業　*shōkōgyō*, commerce and industry
商 社　*shōsha*, trading company
商 店 街　*shōtengai*, shopping street

店　　*ten, mise*

店 員　*ten'in*, clerk
店 主　*tenshu*, shopkeeper
開 店　*kaiten*, (grand) opening of shop

屋　　*ya, oku*

屋 外　*okugai*, outdoors
屋 上　*okujō*, roof (of building)
屋 内　*okunai*, indoors
屋 敷　*yashiki*, mansion

薬　　*yaku, kusuri*

薬 箱　*kusuri-bako*, medicine box
薬 指　*kusuri yubi*, ring finger
薬 品　*yakuhin*, medicines
薬 用　*yakuyō*, medicinal use
薬 剤　*yakuzai*, medicine

化　　*ka, ke, ba, baka(su), bake(ru), ka(suru)*

化 学　*kagaku*, chemistry
お 化 け　*obake*, goblin

品　　*hin, shina*

品 質　*hinshitsu*, quality
品 切 れ　*shinagire*, out of stock
品 物　*shinamono*, goods

容　　yō, katachi

容 易　yōi, simple
容 器　yōki, container
容 積　yōseki, capacity,
　　　volume

院　　in

院 長　inchō, director
大 学 院　daigakuin, graduate
　　　school
参 議 院　Sangiin, House of
　　　Councilors
衆 議 院　Shūgiin, House of
　　　Representatives

髪　　hatsu/-patsu, kami

髪 型　kamigata, hairdo
髪 飾　kami kazari, hair orna-
　　　ment
散 髪　sanpatsu, haircut
洗 髪　senpatsu, shampoo

湯　　tō, yu

湯 治 場　tōjiba, health resort
湯沸かし　yuwakashi, teakettle
秘 湯　hitō, secret hot spring
名 湯　meitō, well-known hot
　　　spring

銭　　sen, zeni

銭 箱　zeni-bako, cash box
小 銭　kozeni, small change
さ い 銭　saisen, monetary
　　　offering

27: CLOTHES

服　　fuku

服 装　fukusō, garments
制 服　seifuku, uniform
和 服　wafuku, Japanese
　　　clothes

供　　ku, kyō, tomo/-domo

供 給　kyōkyū, supply
提 供　teikyō, offer

婦　　fu

婦 長　fuchō, head nurse
婦 人 科　fujinka, gynecology
婦 人 用　fujinyō, for ladies
夫 婦　fūfu, husband and wife
看 護 婦　kangofu, nurse
主 婦　shufu, housewife

士　　shi

学 士　gakushi, university
　　　graduate
計 理 士　keirishi, public ac-
　　　countant

呉　　go, ku(reru)

呉 服 物　gofuku mono, piece/
　　　dry goods

靴　　kutsu, ka

靴 箆　kutsubera, shoehorn
靴 紐　kutsuhimo, shoelace
靴 直 し　kutsu naoshi, shoe
　　　repair
靴 下　kutsushita, sock, stock-
　　　ing
靴 底　kutsuzoko, shoe sole

28: SOME LUXURIES

器　　ki, utsuwa

器 具　kigu, utensil
陶 器　tōki, ceramics

具　　gu

具 合　guai, condition
具 体 的　gutaiteki, definite

167

計　　*kei, haka(ru)*

計画　*keikaku*, plan, project
計画案　*keikakuan*, blueprint
計器　*keiki*, meter, gauge
計算　*keisan*, computation
計算器　*keisanki*, calculator
統計　*tōkei*, statistics
設計　*sekkei*, plan, design

写　　*sha, utsu(su)*

写実　*shajitsu*, realism

真　　*shin, ma*

真冬　*mafuyu*, midwinter
真面目　*majime*, serious
真っ赤　*makka*, deep red
真っ黒　*makkuro*, jet black
真ん中　*mannaka*, center
真夏　*manatsu*, midsummer
真っ直ぐ　*massugu*, straight
真珠　*shinju*, pearl

29: SOME HOBBIES

楽　　*gaku, raku, tano(shii)*

楽団　*gakudan*, orchestra
楽観的　*rakkanteki*, optimistic
楽園　*rakuen*, pleasure garden

書　　*sho, ka(ku)*

書道　*shodō*, calligraphy
書斎　*shosai*, study
書類　*shorui*, document

骨　　*kotsu, hone*

骨折　*kossetsu*, bone fracture
骨つぎ　*honetsugi*, bonesetting

古　　*ko, furu(i)*

古本屋　*furuhon'ya*, used-book store
古里　*furusato*, hometown
古伝　*koden*, legend
古典　*koten*, classics

術　　*jutsu*

技術者　*gijutsusha*, engineer
手術　*shujutsu*, surgical operation

30: FOOD FOR YOUR TABLE

刺身　*sashimi*, sliced raw fish

魚　　*gyo, sakana, uo*

魚介類　*gyokairui*, assorted fishes and shellfishes
魚釣り　*sakana tsuri*, fishing
魚市場　*uo ichiba*, fish market

乳　　*nyū, chi, chichi*

乳房　*chibusa*, breasts
乳製品　*nyūseihin*, dairy products

八　　*ya, hachi*

八方　*happō*, all sides
八重桜　*yae-zakura*, double blossom cherry

果　　*ka, kuda, ha(tasu)*

果実　*kajitsu*, fruit, nut, berry
果汁　*kajū*, fruit juice
果肉　*kaniku*, flesh of fruit
結果　*kekka*, result
効果　*kōka*, effectiveness

Bibliography

Kokumin Hyakka Jiten. Tokyo: Heibonsha, 1968.

Morohashi, Tetsuji. *Kan-Wa Daijiten*. Tokyo: Taishūkan Shoten, 1976.

Kobayashi, Shinmei. *Shinsen Kan-Wa Jiten*. Tokyo: Shōgakukan, 1975.

Nelson, Andrew N. *The Modern Reader's Japanese-English Character Dictionary*, 2nd rev. ed. Tokyo: Charles E. Tuttle Co., 1974.

Nishio, Minoru; Etsutarō Iwabuchi & Shizuo Mizutani eds. *Iwanami Kokugo Jiten*. Tokyo: Iwanami Shoten, 1975.

Onoe, Kanehide ed. *Shōgakusei no tame no Kanji o Oboeru Jiten*. Tokyo, Ōbunsha, 1977.

Shimomura, Noboru. *Kanji no Hon: Ichinensei kara Rokunensei made*. Tokyo: Kaiseisha, 1977.

Shinmura, Izuru ed. *Kōjien*. Tokyo: Iwanami Shoten, 1974.

Shōgaku, Toshiyo ed. *Atarashii Kokugo no Hyōki*. Tokyo: Shōkagukan, 1981.

Takayanagi, Mitsutoshi & Rizo Takeuchi eds. *Nihonshi Jiten*. Tokyo: Kadokawa Shoten, 1974.

Tani, Shin'ichi & Seiroku Noma eds. *Nihon Bijutsu Jiten*. Tokyo: Tōkyōdō Shuppan, 1971.

Yamada, Katsumi. *Kanji no Gogen*. Tokyo: Kadokawa Shoten, 1976.

Pronunciation Index

aji, 98
annaijo, 50, 62
anshin, 62
anshō bangō, 130
atarashii, 26
atatakai, 73

ba, 38
benjo, 35
bentō, 111
bijutsukan, 84
bīru, 108
biyōin, 138
budōshu, 108
Bukkyō, 77
bunbōguya 146
bungaku, 147
bunka, 147
buta, 103
butaniku no shōgayaki, 103
Butsu, 78
butsu, 85, 151
byōin, 138

cha, 110
chāhan, 95
cha no yu, 111
chāshūmen, 95
chiisai, 53
chikai, 39
chikara, 36

chikatetsu sen, 42
chirashi-zushi, 107
chō, 91
chū-gata, 53
Chūgoku (Chūka) ryōri, 93
Chūkadon, 102
Chūkajinmin Kyōwakoku, 93
Chūka soba, 94
chūō, 22, 119
Chūō Sen, 37

Daibutsu, 79
daiyokujō, 69
de-guchi, 21
denki, 132
denki kigu, 142
denkiryō, 132
denki ten, 141–2
densha, 32
denwa, 132
denwaryō, 132
Doitsu ryōri, 94
donburi, 101
dorai karē, 103

Edo-jō, 82
Edomae-zushi, 107
Eidan Sen, 43
eigyōchū, 112
eki, 19
en, 92, 130

ēroguramu, 117
eyaretā, 117

fu, 116
fujin, 140
fuku, 140
Furansu ryōri, 94
furuhon'ya, 148
furui, 148
fūtō, 120
futoi, 87
futon, 63
futsū, 33, 123

gaijin, 25
gaikoku kawase, 124
gakki ten, 145
gei, 147
genkin kakitome, 120
gin, 31, 121
ginkō, 121
Ginza Sen, 31
gofuku ten, 140
gohan, 103
gomoku soba, 94
go-nyūkin, 123
gūji, 77
guratin, 103
gurīnken, 50
gyūniku no shōgayaki, 103
gyūnyūya, 150

hagaki, 117
hai/-bai/-pai, 109
haikanryū, 80
hakubutsukan, 84
haku/-paku, 65
hama, 75
hamu, 103

hanbāgā sutēki, 103
hassha, 34
hatsu/-patsu, 34
heijitsu, 56, 115
hi, 56
hidari, 24
hidari gawa tsūkō, 23
higashi, 21, 28
hikidashi, 124
hikkoshi soba, 96
hikōki, 59
hiragana, 23, 106
hiyashi Chūka, 93
Hokkaidō, 86, 116
hōmen, 26, 32
hon, 146
hon/-bon/-pon, 109
honjitsu, 113
Honshū, 86
hon'ya, 137, 146
hōseki ten, 143
Hotoke, 78
hyaku, 90

ichi, 65, 91
Ikebukuro, 28
in, 138
inari-zushi, 107
inoko, 103
ippaku nishoku tsuki, 65
iri-guchi, 21
iwashi, 106

ji, 56, 143
jidō hikidashiki, 125
jidō sābisuki, 125
jingū, 77
jinja, 76
jitsu, 56

jō, 82
Jōetsu, 37
Jōyō Kanji, 101
junbichū, 113
junkyū, 33

kabayaki, 105
kādo, 128
kadō sōnyū-guchi, 130
kagu ten, 143
kai, 74
kaigan, 74
kaisatsu-guchi, 21
kaisha/-gaisha, 58, 61
kaisō, 54
kaisoku, 33
kajū, 151
kakitome, 120
kaku, 146
kaku eki teisha, 33
kakunin, 131
kamera ten, 144
kami, 76, 139
kamikaze, 52
kampai, 109
kanai, 25, 70
kane, 40
kankō, 62
kankō annaijo, 60
kannushi, 77
kasasagi, 144
kashiya, 151
kasshu sābisu kōnā, 125
katachi, 138
kata/-gata, 53
katakana, 99, 117
katsudon, 102
kawa/-gawa, 27, 71
kawase, 124

kaze, 70
kazoku, 70
kazoku buro, 69
kazu, 49
ken, 39, 49
keshōhin ten, 137
keshō shitsu, 138
ki, 47, 59, 126
ki, 71, 87
kin, 40, 66, 121
kinen kitte, 117
kingaku, 134
kingaku botan, 42
kinkyori kippu, 39
kinyū, 129
kippu, 38
kissaten, 110, 111
kita, 22
kitsuen shitsu, 110
kitte, 117
ko, 73
kobijutsuhin ten, 148
kodomo, 39, 40, 42, 140
kōen, 61
ko-gata, 53
kōhī, 111
koin rokka, 51
kojin takushī, 54
kōka, 47
koka-kōra, 111
kokoa, 111
koku, 30, 72
kōkū-gaisha, 58
Kokuhō, 80, 82
kokuritsu kōen, 72
Kokusai Yūbin Kyoku, 119
kōkūshokan, 117
Kokutetsu, 30, 37, 42
kōkyo, 83

kome, 94, 137
kondo no densha, 51
kondo no hassha, 33
koromo, 101
kōsha, 61
kotobuki, 106
kōtsū, 61
kottōhin ten, 147
kōza bangō, 123
kozutsumi, 118
kuchi/-guchi, 20
kudamonoya, 151
kudari, 34
kujira, 106
kuni, 30
kurīmu sōda, 111
kuruma, 32
kūsha, 53
kusuri, 98, 137
kutsu ten, 141
kyoku, 119, 137
Kyōto-fu, 116
kyūgyō, 114
kyūjitsu, 56, 115
kyūkō, 33
Kyūshū, 87

mai, 41, 90
matsuri, 119
me, 23, 28
medamayaki, 105
michi, 76
midori no madoguchi, 39, 49
migi, 24
migi gawa tsūkō, 23
mikkusu piza, 103
minami, 21
minato, 58
mingeihin ten, 147

mingeikan, 85
minshuku, 63
mise, 111, 137
mizuumi, 73
mono, 85, 151
mori, 71
mori soba, 96

nabeyaki udon, 97
nai, 25, 62
naka, 22
nama bīru, 108
nama-yasai, 109
nama-zakana, 109
Narita, 57
nichi, 56
nigiri-zushi, 107
Nihon, 60
Nihon Kai, 74, 87
Nihon Kōkū, 58
Nihon Kōtsū Kōsha, 60
Nihon ryōri, 94
Nihonshu, 108, 152
Nihon soba, 95
niku, 103
nikuya, 150
ningen, 80
Ningen Kokuhō, 80
Nippon Denshin-Denwa, 134
Nippon Hōsō Kyōkai, 134
nishi, 22
niwa, 81
nobori, 22, 34
noriba, 32
norikae, 32
nori-maki, 107
nyōbō, 147
nyū, 39, 150
nyūjōken, 39, 42

o-azuke ire, 129
obōsan, 78
o-cha, 111
ō-gata, 53
o-hikidashi, 124, 129
okonomiyaki, 105
oku, 91, 137
omoi 148
omote, 67
onna, 36, 68
onsen, 72
orenji jūsu, 111
Ōsaka-fu, 116
Ōsaka-jō, 82
Ōsaka-zushi, 107
o-senbe, 152
o-shiharai, 128
o-shinko-maki, 107
o-tearai, 35, 67
otoko, 35, 68
otona, 42
o-toriatsukaichū, 128
otsuri, 42
owari, 113
oya, 101
ōyake, 61
oyako donburi, 101

raisu, 103
rāmen, 94
restoran, 99
rihatsu ten, 138
riyō ten, 138
ryō, 46
ryōgae, 41, 126
ryokan, 63
ryōkin, 66
ryokō-gaisha, 60
ryōshū kingaku, 134

ryōshūshō, 133
ryōte, 126

sābisu ranchi, 103
sakaba, 108
sakana, 106
sakanaya, 149
sakaya, 108, 152
sake, 107, 152
sanpatsuya, 138
San'yō, 37
sashimi, 149
sashimi teishoku, 100
satsu, 40, 46
seikyūsho, 133
seiriken, 57
seisanjo, 36
sekitei, 81
sen, 29
sen, 47
sen, 90
sen'en, 40
senmenjo, 35, 66
sennin buro, 69
sentō, 47, 139
Setonai Kai, 74
shakai, 61
shashin ten, 144
shibui, 27
Shibuya, 27
shihei tōnyū-guchi, 131
Shikoku, 87
shima/-jima, 75
shina, 27, 138
Shinagawa, 27
shindaiken, 50
Shinjuku, 26
Shinkan Sen, 37
shinshi, 140

Shintō, 76
Shin Tōkyō Kokusai Kūkō, 57
shiro, 82
shiso-maki, 107
shitagi, 140
shiteiken, 49
shiyō chūshi, 128
shōchū, 108, 152
shoku, 65, 100
shokudō, 99
shokuryōhin ten, 153
shōnin yado, 63
shōten, 136
shoten, 137, 146
shukuba, 20, 26
shukuhaku ryōkin, 65
shūryū shimashita, 113
shūyūken, 50
soba, 95–96
sōdan, 122
sokutatsu, 120
sora, 58
sōryo, 78
soto mawari, 25
subuta, 95
suidō kyoku, 134
sukiyaki, 105
sūpāmāketto, 153
supōtsu yōhin, 145
sushiya, 104

ta, 58
ta, 116
ta-fu-ken, 116
Taiheiyō, 87
takushī noriba, 52
tamago, 102
tamagodon, 102
tamago-maki, 107

tanmen, 95
tanoshii, 145
tare, 104
te, 35
tearai, 34
teien, 81
teikiken, 48
teiki yokin, 125
teikyūbi, 114
teiryūjo, 55
teisei, 130
teishoku, 99
tekka-maki, 107
tempura, 97
tempura teishoku, 100
ten, 111, 137
tendon, 102
tenrankai, 85
teppanyaki, 105
tera/-dera, 78
tetsu, 30, 105
teuchi soba, 96
teuchi udon, 97
Toei Basu, 55
Toei Sen, 45
Toei Sen renraku, 45
Tōhoku, 37
Tokaidō, 37
tokei ten, 143
toki, 56, 143
tokkyū, 33
tokkyūken, 50
tokoro, 36, 67
tokoya, 138
Tōkyō, 28
Tōkyō Chūō Yūbin Kyoku, 119
Tōkyō Denryoku, 134
Tōkyō Gasu, 134
Tōkyō-to, 115

tonkatsu teishoku, 100
tōnyū kingaku, 40
tori, 104
torikeshi, 40, 44, 131
toshikoshi soba, 95
tsūchō, 123, 128
tsugi no hassha, 33
tsuki, 65
tsuyu, 97

uchi mawari, 25
udon, 95, 97
Ueno, 28
uisukī, 108
uma, 19
umi, 74
unadon, 105
unagi, 105
undōgu ten, 146
uranai, 111
uriba, 38
urikire, 114
ushi, 103
utsuwa, 142
utsukushii, 84

wa-gashi, 152
wain, 108
wantanmen, 95
wasuremono uketamawarijo, 51

wasureru, 51

yaki soba, 94, 105
yakitoriya, 104
yakkyoku, 137
yaku, 98, 137
yakumi, 98
yama, 71
Yamanote Sen, 24, 37
yaoya, 150
yasai, 150
yobidashi, 44, 47, 131
yōfuku ten, 140
yō-gashi, 152
yōhin ten, 140
yokin, 123
yoku shitsu, 68
yoyaku, 66
yu, 139
yubi, 49
yūbin, 116
yūbin posuto, 115
yuki, 32

zandaka shōkai, 129
zaru soba, 96
zei, 135
zeikin, 134
zensen, 43
zō, 79

Index

account number, 123, 125
admission fee, 80
adult ticket, 42
air letter, 117
airline company, 58
Akihabara, 142
Amaterasu Ōmikami, 76, 77
antiques, 147
art museum, 84
automatic teller machine (ATM),
    121, 125, 127, 131
automatic transfer, 133

bank account, 123
bankbook, 122, 125, 128, 130
banking hours, 121
barbershop, 138
bargaining, 54
beach, 75
beauty shop, 138
beef, 103, 150
beer, 108
bill, 133
boarding area, 32
book store, 137
bound for, 32
box lunch, 110
Buddha, 78

cancel, 40, 44, 131
cash card, 125, 128, 130

cash dispenser (CD), 121
change machine, 42, 126
chicken, 104, 150
child's ticket, 42
China, 87, 93, 95, 116
Chinese restaurant, 93, 94
Chūō Line, 37
clock/watch, 143
closed for the day, 114
coffee shop, 110
commemorative stamp, 117
commuter pass, 48
confectioneries, 151
confirmation, 131
consultation, 122
correction, 130
cosmetics, 137
counter -hai/-bai/-pai, 109;
    haku/-paku, 65; -hon/-bon/-
    pon, 109; mai, 90
coupon ticket, 48, 49
current balance, 129

daily special, 99
deposit, 123, 128, 129, 131
drugstore, 137

east, 21
Edo, 107
Edo Castle, 31, 82
eel, 105

Eidan Lines, 42
electric appliance, 142
electric bill, 132
entrance/exit, 19–21
excursion ticket, 50
express, 33
express ticket, 49

family bath, 69
fare adjustment, 36
fee, 66, 133
first class, 49, 50
fish, 102, 106, 149
fixed term deposit, 125
folk art/craft, 85, 147
foreign exchange, 124
French cuisine, 94
fruit juice, 151
furniture, 142

garnish, 98
gas company, 134
Ginza Line, 31
going down/up, 23
Gotō Art Museum, 84
Great Buddha, 79
green window, 39, 49

hand-beaten noodles, 96
Haneda Airport, 58
Heian Jingū, 77
Hokkaidō, 86, 116
Honshū, 37, 86
Hōryūji, 77
hot spring, 69, 72

Ikebukuro, 24, 25, 28
Imperial Palace, 28, 31, 83
information office, 50, 62, 64

inner circle, 25
in service, 128
island, 75
Izu, 73

Japan, 60
Japanese Archipelago, 86
Japanese National Railways, 24, 29, 45
Japan Travel Bureau, 60, 64
Jōyō Kanji, 101, 148

keep left/right, 23
kimono, 140
Korea, 87, 95
Kōshū Highway, 26, 63, 64
Kurita Art Museum, 84
Kyoto, 148
Kyoto Prefecture, 116
Kyushu, 87

lake, 73
left, 24
line, 25, 29
liquor store, 108, 152
Living National Treasure, 80
local train, 33
long distance ticket, 48, 49
lost and found office, 51

Marunouchi Line, 31
meat, 102, 103, 149
medicine, 98, 137
Meiji Jingū, 77
men, 35, 68
milk, 150
MOA Museum of Art, 84
money, 40, 66
mountain, 71

Mount Fuji, 25, 71, 73

Nara, 79
Narita Airport, 58
National Museum of Western Art, 84
National Museums, 84
national park, 72
National Treasure, 80, 82, 117
New Tokyo International Airport, 57
New Trunk Lines, 37
Noboribetsu, 73
north, 21, 86

Ohara Art Museum, 84
ordinary, 33
ordinary account, 123, 124
Osaka, 37, 142
Osaka Castle, 82
Osaka Prefecture, 116
outdoor bath, 70
outer circle, 25
out of service, 128
owner-driver, 54

Pacific Ocean, 74, 87
park, 61
People's Republic of China, 93
platform ticket, 38
pork, 103, 150
postal savings, 119
postcard, 117
powder room, 138
prefecture, 86, 116
preparing to open, 113
process of, 113
public bathhouse, 47, 139
public broadcasting fee, 134

raw fish, 109, 149
receipt, 133
registered cash, 120
regular day of rest, 114
rental locker, 51
reservation, 60, 66
reserved seat, 49
rice, 103
right, 24
river, 27, 71
road, 76
Ryukyu Archipelago, 86

sake, 107, 152
schedule, 56
sea, 74, 86
seacoast, 74
Sea of Japan, 74, 87
secret ID number, 125, 130
semiexpress, 33
set-fare system, 57
Shibuya, 24, 27, 38
Shikoku, 87
Shinagawa, 25, 27
Shinjuku, 24, 25, 26, 64
shop/store, 111, 136
short distance ticket, 38
Shōtoku Taishi, 77
shrine, 75, 76, 77
sleeping car ticket, 50
sold out, 114
south, 21
special delivery, 120
special express, 33
special express ticket, 49, 50
sporting goods, 145
stamp, 117
stuffed pancake, 105
subway line, 30, 42

sukiyaki, 105
supermarket, 149, 153
suspension of business, 114

tax, 68, 134
taxi stand, 52
tea ceremony, 111
telephone bill/call, 132
telephone company, 134
temple, 75, 78
Three Treasures, 77
ticket, 23, 39, 49
ticket gate, 21, 36
tipping, 54, 68
Tōdaiji, 79
Toei Bus, 55
Toei Lines, 42, 45
toilet, 34, 67
Tokugawa Ieyasu, 83
Tokyo, 24, 28, 37, 83, 94
Tokyo Central Post Office, 117, 119
Tokyo International Post Office, 119
Tokyo Metropolitan Prefecture, 115

training gear, 146
transfer, 32
transfer ticket, 45
travel agency, 60, 64

Ueno, 25, 28
up/down train, 34
urban prefecture, 116

vacancy indicator, 54
vegetables, 150

water bureau, 134
weekday, 56, 115
west, 21, 22
Western clothes/goods, 140
whiskey, 108
wine, 108
withdrawal, 123, 128, 129
women, 35, 68

Yamanote Line, 24, 26, 29, 37, 51
yen, 92

Zen, 78